# Praise for *Love in a Time of Crisis*

"Vivian's book is not only a wonderful guide for those in challenging times but a treasure of wisdom for all who open its pages and their hearts."

—Dave Ellingson, adventurer, author, and speaker

"A must-read for those facing the end-of-life journey either for themselves or for a friend or loved one. How rare it is to read an account that discusses with complete truthfulness the joys, sorrows, pains, and hopes of the journey that awaits us all."

—Robert Hilton, PhD, author of *Relational Somatic Psychotherapy*

"This lovely book should be required reading for my nursing colleagues as it will give them insight into the challenges of caring not only for the patient but also for the family."

—Janet Evans Emery, retired RN, MSN, Family Nurse Practitioner

"This insightful memoir offers solace to those who have experienced Alzheimer's disease and its effect on others."

—Ashley Croslin, Director of Wellness Programs, Regents Point

"What a treasure this book is. Vivian provides a rare glimpse into the soul of the caregiving journey. With insight and stunning transparency, she carries us into the depth of hardship and back into the light of tender possibilities. By generously sharing her love, strength, and courage, she inspires readers to find their own."
—Corby Beahm, MS, RN

"Vivian's words are an honest reflection of grief and hardship and yet leave you embedded in a love story that is stronger than death. She will take you on a deeply moving journey."
—Anne Hoang, BSN, RN, ACM

"Having served as a parish pastor for more than fifty years, I highly recommend *Love in a Time of Crisis* for all theological students and others preparing for a life of service."
—Hub Nelson, Pastor, Evangelical Lutheran
  Church in America

"As a hospice social worker, I find Vivian's narrative a refreshing balance we all seek while juggling the redefinition of hope, purpose, and meaning as we care for a loved one."
—Gregory Rice, MSW, hospice, geriatric,
  and medical social worker

*To my [friend, Hub?]
journey mercies.
May you be held
in the light of
God's love

With my love
and appreciation,

Vivian Elaine*

# Love in a Time of Crisis

*A Message of Hope
for Caregivers and Others*

Vivian Elaine Johnson

SUMMIT RUN PRESS

Summit Run Press
www.summitrunpress.com

"The Map You Make Yourself" excerpt © Jan Richardson from *Circle of Grace: A Book of Blessings for the Seasons*. Used by permission, janrichardson.com.

Ordering Information
Quantity sales. Special discounts are available on quantity purchases by corporations, associations, and others. For details, contact the "Special Sales Department" at the address above.

Orders by US trade bookstores and wholesalers. Please contact BCH: (800) 431-1579 or visit www.bookch.com for details.

Printed in the United States of America

Cataloging-in-Publication Data

Names: Johnson, Vivian Elaine, author.
Title: Love in a time of crisis : a message of hope for caregivers and others / Vivian Elaine Johnson.
Description: Irvine, CA: Summit Run Press, 2021.
Identifiers: LCCN: 2021906999 | ISBN: 978-0-9987689-7-7
Subjects: LCSH Johnson, Vivian Elaine. | Caregivers--Biography. | Caregivers--Conduct of life.
Alzheimer's disease--Patients--Care. | Alzheimer's disease--Patients--Home care--Psychological aspects. | Alzheimer's disease--Patients--Family relationships. | BISAC FAMILY & RELATIONSHIPS / Life Stages / Later Years | SELF-HELP / Motivational & Inspirational
Classification: LCC RC523 .J64 2021 | DDC 362.6092--dc23

First Edition

25 24 23 22 21     10 9 8 7 6 5 4 3 2 1

*In memory of my husband,*
*George Severin Johnson,*
*and my son, Todd,*
*whose spirits infuse each page.*
*In honor of my daughters,*
*Sonja and Joy,*
*whose spirits sustain me.*

# *Contents*

# *Preface*

FOR TEN YEARS, MY husband lived with several health issues. The last two years of his life, a diagnosis of Alzheimer's was added to the list. I was his primary caregiver.

To preserve my sanity, gain balance, and cope, I got out my laptop and began to write, usually early in the morning. My writing culminated in this book, which opens the door to our experience: our vulnerabilities and insecurities as well as the positive and loving moments we shared. It upholds our belief in the resilience of human beings.

In life with my husband, I knew my role. I was introduced to others as "George's lovely wife." We married in a time of male dominance, at least in the circles in which we lived. George called me his helpmate, a Biblical term. I was to help him accomplish his goals. That was fine, but I always wanted to be more. After sixty years in that role, however, my "place" was etched in the stone of my psyche. George became an advocate for women's rights but sometimes found it difficult to practice that in his personal life. Though he was always kind, his schedule, his work, and his seven books all took first place, leading me to believe that he was more important than I. While I managed to accomplish some things that I'm proud of—motherhood, my education, my profession—it all took second place to being George's helpmate. During the years of his declining health, I began to move past that thinking.

Observing the physical and mental changes in my husband over the years was painful. My academic and professional background is in behavioral science with a focus on dealing with loss. As medical people can tell you, their expertise helps patients; however, when the patient is their loved one, it is a different situation as an emotional element enters. My knowledge and experience around the topic of loss were helpful, but this time it was different indeed because the client was my husband. George's losses—and mine—were numerous. Writing helped me sort out my reactions and feelings. I believe it also helped me be a better caregiver—and person.

In the midst of this personal and marital crisis, our world was turned upside down due to the invasion of an international pandemic, COVID-19. It stormed into all lives, including ours. We wore face masks and were physically distanced from friends and family. Such isolation impacted George and me at a time when support was so important to our physical, mental, and emotional stability. As if the pandemic weren't enough, our country, the *United* States of America, became politically *disunited*. It was disheartening and frightening to witness such an absence of national unity. We also saw the killing of several African Americans by police officers, which resulted in protests throughout the country. All of these events caused collective trauma. Consequently, our personal crisis was complicated by the national and international crises.

In this book I reveal difficulties but also the beauty and love George and I experienced on our journey. I share these writings with you with the intention of encouraging you, especially in your times of crisis. I hope that as you read this book you find the love and hope that was tucked in the cracks and crevices of our days. May you be strengthened and find peace in whatever journey you are on.

When you pass through the
    waters, I will be with you;
and through the rivers, they
    shall not overwhelm you.
—Isaiah 43:2

# *Introduction:* THE MAN

PEOPLE WHO KNEW GEORGE well appropriately described him as a strong-willed person. Yet that strength was hidden behind a quiet, humble, and calm personality. He could be characterized as a steel fist in a velvet glove.

His profession was that of clergyman, one to which he was well suited. He sensed a call to living his life in the service of God. About twenty years into his career, he was deeply moved by the plight of marginalized people in our world: those in poverty and those treated unequally because of their race, gender, sexual orientation, or class. Ministry on behalf of them became his focus. His strong will was a valuable resource in the face of opposition by many, including people of faith.

When George and I met in our midtwenties, I saw the velvet glove but had no knowledge of or experience with the steel fist, the strong-willed man. It began to show itself when George chose to marry me. I was a divorcee with a young child—a fabulous child, I might add. The national church said, "No, you can't marry a divorced woman and still be a pastor." My first husband was a sociopath, but the church was not interested in why I was divorced. Its decision was a slap in George's face after his nine years of post–high school education to become a pastor. The church said, "Final decision."

I did not want the responsibility or the reputation of ruining George's career, so I believed we should not marry. However, because George was a strong-willed, think-outside-the-box person, and we loved each other, we married. His determination paid off: two years later the church changed its mind. It began to evaluate each request for ordination on its own merits. George went on to serve the church and the disenfranchised for over fifty years—with me at his side.

We were walking back to our apartment one April evening after dinner in our community's dining room. The air was calm and balmy with a gentle aroma of spring blossoms. Since George's walking was precarious and we were walking down a slight decline, he tightly held onto my arm. Without warning, he fell to the pavement, pulling me down with him. I could smell the asphalt as my head jerked back and bounced on the hard surface. I reached back and felt a large bump and then saw blood on my fingers. I managed to sit up and saw George lay unmoving on the pavement in front of me. Fear shivered down my spine. George needed help. I crawled at first, then stood and shakily walked back to the dining room. To my relief, people immediately came to my assistance.

Within minutes, two ambulances arrived, one for George and one for me. We were taken to a trauma center because of my head injury. The care was swift. I remember that the emergency room staff wanted to cut off my shirt. I objected—I liked that shirt!—and said it could be pulled over my wounded head. Tests showed that my injury was not internal (I just had a grapefruit-sized lump on the back of my head) so my breathing calmed. I was discharged and allowed to go see George in a nearby room. When I arrived, he was arguing with a nurse, claiming he didn't need to be x-rayed, despite having severe pain in his hip.

My irritation rose as I listened to his stubborn resistance. Our two daughters arrived, and with our unified urging, George finally consented to x-rays. He had a broken hip and was scheduled for surgery the next day. Following his surgery and hospital stay, he was transferred to a rehab facility and then to assisted living. After seven weeks he was well enough to return to our apartment. He and I were so pleased that he was finally where he loved to be—settled in at home.

Then, something happened.

# *1.* THE NEWS

THE NEUROLOGIST IN HER starched white coat said, "We have the results of your extensive neurological tests." She looked with a steady gaze into George's eyes. "They conclude that you have dementia." She paused as she waited for this news to sink in. "We suspected so, but now we have the proof." I noticed that she was beautiful. How could such disturbing news come from one so lovely?

"Do I have Alzheimer's?" George asked in a small, husky voice.

"Yes," she replied. The kindness expressed in her face comforted me. At least the bearer of bad news delivered it with gentleness. I heard it; I didn't hear it. I believed it; I didn't believe it.

"What should I do?" George asked, appearing somewhat perplexed.

"Nothing," she responded with a beauteous smile. "Keep enjoying your life by being active socially, physically, and mentally."

"Enjoy each moment? Each day?" I inquired. My throat was dry.

"Yes," the neurologist affirmed, "do as your wife suggests, George. Enjoy each day."

George sat quietly for a while and then asked, "What will happen?"

"Your memory will gradually get worse," she responded in an even, unemotional tone. I felt a chill. The room seemed too sterile, harsh, and bright. There was no softness.

"Will I die from it?"

"You will not die from Alzheimer's. It doesn't kill people, but complications can."

In the car on our way home, I noticed children playing in a park, laughing. How could anyone be happy when our news was so sad? While we were going through a personal crisis, it was astounding to discover that the rest of the world was going on as usual. How dare it continue as if nothing had happened? After all, my personal world had flown off its axis.

I looked over at George, whose face showed no expression. I wanted to discuss the test results with him yet not be intrusive. I thought I should respect his need to process. Finally, I ventured, "How is this for you?"

My question hung in the air. George looked straight ahead and said, "She didn't beat around the bush. She was very frank."

"Yes, I'm glad she had the courage to tell us the truth. Now we know what we're dealing with."

George nodded, still showing no emotion. My heartbeat was rapid. I reminded myself to be calm, to drive carefully. "I'm here for you, sweetheart," I said as I reached for his hand. "I'll be with you all the way."

"Thank you," he said. George was quiet. Finally, he asked, "When did this start?"

"About four years ago I saw some beginning signs," I responded. "As the neurologist said, it's more evident to the person closest to you than it is to you yourself. I noticed several behavior issues—and memory loss. Two years ago, you were diagnosed with mild cognitive impairment. Now that diagnosis has changed to Alzheimer's." I noticed that I didn't like to say the word.

Neither did George. He said, "*Dementia* sounds better."

In our silence, I recalled the words of author Faith Baldwin: "Time is a dressmaker, specializing in alterations." We have been altered, all right—both the man I married and his wife.

We arrived home. George went immediately to lie down in the bedroom. I looked at the description of his new medication:

Memantine is used to treat moderate to severe confusion (dementia) related to Alzheimer's disease. It does not cure Alzheimer's disease, but it may improve memory, awareness, and the ability to perform daily functions. This medicine works by blocking the action of a certain natural substance in the brain (glutamate) that is believed to be linked to symptoms of Alzheimer's disease.

Tears came easily. My strongest response was sadness. I was sad for George, sad for our children and grandchildren, sad for extended family and friends, and, yes, sad for myself.

My apprehension rose: what next? Am I going to be able to cope with this? Am I capable of being his daily caregiver? How many years do we have left? Will I live long enough to care for him? I was reminded of something I read, "Always carry a dream in your heart. It will keep you warm on cold days." On this emotionally chilly day, my dream was that we become other-focused as opposed to self-focused. With bad news, it is easy to become self-absorbed. Also, my dream was that we intentionally look for the beauty in little things so our souls would be blessed with inner peace. Was that too positive a spin? I needed it. That is how I cope.

In the midst of sadness and apprehension, life goes on. I glanced at our patio. A single yellow rose stood tall and gorgeous as it reached for the sun. Thank you, rose, for reminding me to look for the beauty in each day.

# 2. Is This My Man?

AWAKE AT NIGHT, I stared at the darkness, fear lapping at the edges of my heart. I told myself to be optimistic but also realistic. What did the future hold? Our marriage, this closest of relationships, was being invaded by an intruder. Was it an enemy?

As the days moved on and I tried to adjust to this unwanted news, I found that I had a few questions. Okay, maybe one hundred. I turned to Siri on my iPhone, my new best friend. "How can I help?" she asked. (Talk about an offer!) "Siri, what is the definition of *overwhelmed*?"

From her trove of information, that Library of Congress in her teeny-weeny head, she replied. "*Overwhelmed* is to bury or drown beneath a huge mass; inundate; have a strong emotional effect on." (How does Siri do that?)

Why was I feeling overwhelmed—that is, buried, inundated, and yes, experiencing strong emotions? It was because I had so many questions and decisions to make in living with a beloved person who has Alzheimer's. Questions loomed, ones that not even Siri could answer. In regard to my husband and some of his new behaviors,

I wondered, Who *are* you? What *are* you doing? How will we manage this? I realized that such questions were not dissimilar from those one may ask after the first year of marriage.

Let's start with "Who *are* you?" He looked pretty much the same. He was a six-footer with long arms and legs. He disliked his freckles, but I was fond of them as they lent a bit of "boy" to his appearance. I'd always liked his hands with long, slim fingers. When we were dating, I remember focusing on them, fascinated. He'd been balding for several years, but he joked that God made some heads so beautiful that they don't need hair to cover them. His appearance was very familiar to me, but other things had changed. Relationships are complicated. George had always been a bit of an enigma to me. (*I* am a bit of an enigma to me.) However, after almost sixty years of knowing and loving him, I thought I was close to figuring him out—until now.

It is important to say that George was still a person of intellect, especially in the subjects in which he had immersed himself throughout the years. He could talk theology and politics. He could express himself and ask intelligent—even brilliant—questions. Visitors said, "He seems fine, like his old self." A friend whose father had Alzheimer's wrote, "My father was very bright, as is your husband, and the neurologist said he probably had many coping strategies that hid the problem until Alzheimer's was more fully developed."

I experienced a new man. Our niece Amy said it well: "He is a different presentation of his former self." He was a man I looked at daily and thought, Who *are* you? The present George was so pronounced that reaching back to recall the George of the past was difficult. Comments by other people helped me. Numerous people remembered that his speaking ability was outstanding; some claimed they recalled portions of his sermons from years ago. A former church member recently wrote, "We heard great sermons week after week after week."

Others credited him with changing their life's direction; his words and actions led them to move from selfish lives to lives given for others. Some worked for the resolution of world hunger. A man who now holds the position George formerly held as world hunger director for our church's national organization recently wrote, "George has moved mountains and altered the pathways of history for good. He has changed hearts and minds and called people to courageously follow the journey of the Holy Spirit in the way of love and justice. He has spoken with authenticity and without hesitation."

His sister Ruth wrote, "Brother, I so honor and respect your outstanding passion for social justice issues. Your books are written so well and they will be studied and learned from even after you get your wings." Other words used to describe George were "relentless," "indefatigable," and "a burr under the saddle"—all true in my experience. "Focused and driven" was another description. Those characteristics are precisely why he accomplished so much. He had the ability to be absorbed in a project, whether it be a sermon, a class, the planning of a conference, or, on a lighter note, a golf or tennis game. With his persuasive and persistent personality, he was able to network and, to the amazement of his colleagues, approach and secure big names to speak at any number of events. "It never hurts to ask" was his mantra.

Some of his characteristics that I knew so well were now changing. For example, one of his major characteristics—the essence of his personality—was his skill of asking questions. He often asked our children and grandchildren, "Did you ask a good question today?" In any social setting it was the same: questions, questions, questions. Surprisingly, he said to me, "I wish people would ask *me* questions at the dining table instead of me always being the one to ask questions."

One evening we decided to have dinner alone in the dining room of the continuing-care facility where we lived—almost like we were on a date. I noticed that George enjoyed reminiscing, and I recalled his comment about wishing others would ask him questions. We'll have some fun, I thought. I'll ask him questions about one of his favorite topics: the churches he served as a pastor over the past fifty years.

During the salad course, between bites of crunchy greens, carrots, and cucumber, I said, "You worked with many organists throughout your ministry, honey. Did you have some favorites?" He appeared to recall quite well, needing only minor help pulling up names.

While enjoying the entrée, I asked about his secretaries, "Who was the most efficient?" and then about the physical buildings, "Did you have a favorite church architecture?" While enjoying his helping of mashed potatoes and gravy, he seemed engaged in the conversation. I was pleased. In recalling the past, we were having a stimulating dinner hour.

That night in bed, George said, "Vivian, you made me uncomfortable at dinner tonight."

"Really? Why?"

"I felt like you were interrogating me! You asked me all those questions."

I was shocked. This from Mr. Questioner, the man who answered questions by asking questions? Go figure. Who *are* you?

In retrospect I realize that even though he wanted to be asked questions, he was more comfortable asking the questions. In being questioned, perhaps he felt inadequate, fearing that he couldn't recall the past. This made him ill at ease and agitated. As he reminded me, "I'm not the man I used to be." I reminded myself that he had a disease, Alzheimer's.

Another of my husband's characteristics was patience. In fact, when he wanted to get his way, he would wait it out patiently until he succeeded. Now he became impatient, which showed up as irritability. At church one day,

George went to the technology booth where a young person graciously assisted hard-of-hearing people. Each Sunday, George would pick up a hearing device to better hear the church service. Suddenly, I heard my once-patient husband say in his loud preacher voice, "Where's the hearing thing? It's not here where it's supposed to be!" His tone was less than kind, more like "you incompetent kid." True, the device wasn't where it usually is; it lay five inches to the left. Who *are* you?

I watched as the filters of speech and action and his inhibitions diminished. Sometimes the result was inappropriate behavior, which could be embarrassing. I attempted to learn how to interact with a dementia patient through various guidelines available in literature. I was told that I needed to embrace three tenets:

1. Don't argue with the person.
2. Refrain from trying to reason.
3. Do not explain.

The first idea didn't seem difficult, as arguing was not my usual method of interacting. However, refraining from reasoning and explaining was a different story. Reasoning and explaining were at the heart of how I thought and conversed, and they were the way I taught our children to interact. They were the way I operated with friends, and how I wrote and spoke. Surely, if I reasoned and explained, most situations could be worked through. I was told that this was not the case when interacting with a person with dementia. I could explain and reason till the cows come home; it was not going to work. Instead, I was told to repeat, distract, or refocus the person.

One of our disagreements happened because George did not want me to lock the house or car. His reason was "it's not necessary." When I locked the door, he said, "What's the matter with you anyway?" I learned not to argue, reason, or explain. Just do it.

Though the answer to "Who are you?" changed frequently, I didn't question my love for this old new man. Somehow in George's current vulnerability, he had endeared himself to me in a way that he couldn't when he was young and physically, mentally, and emotionally strong.

He was still my man.

# *3.* TEARS

IN THE EARLY HOURS, before the gentle morning light peeked into my kitchen, I often sat at the table and pondered life. I appreciated and thrived in that private time. Alzheimer's caused George to sleep for more hours, giving me that luxurious quiet with which to begin the day. That's when I cried. I cried for George and for our son who died long ago.

Tears are helpful when dealing with emotional pain, but anger has a place as well. Sometimes, for women, anger would be the more appropriate reaction, yet we cry. I grew up in a culture where women were not supposed to show anger. "Nice girls are sweet and kind," we were told. Crying was far more acceptable than yelling in anger. But then Esther entered my life. She taught me about the appropriateness of anger. Each day, as I sat by my dying son at City of Hope National Medical Center, I noticed a woman who peeked in the door of Todd's hospital room every time she walked down the hall. Esther was petite with bleached blonde, unruly hair that stuck out in a multitude of directions. Her head looked like a spiky planet attached to a body in perpetual motion.

One day, Esther confronted me in the cafeteria.

"Are you that boy's mother?" She jumped straight in, no hello or introduction of herself.

I hesitated, then said, "Yes."

In a close to abrasive sound, she asked, "What's wrong with him?" She offered no subtlety here either.

I hesitated to give voice to Todd's illness. I felt the devastation and realness of it each time I said it aloud. Yet I also felt the need to be polite. "He is seriously ill with rhabdomyosarcoma, an aggressive cancer."

Esther's sharp dark eyes pierced my wet blue eyes, and she said, "Shit!"

Her word of anger jolted me. It opened some closed compartment inside of me, giving me permission to be angry—and better yet, permission to express that anger. Though I wouldn't have used her word, Esther voiced the raw truth. I found it refreshing. She didn't say, as some did, "Todd looks much better today," as I watched my son deteriorate before my eyes.

Esther and I had frank conversations from that day forward. I knew I could tell her the worst. I could fume and cry, even sob. I didn't have to protect her. She and I both knew that it was a shitty situation.

We became so close that when her husband died, she wanted George and me at the memorial service. She asked George to participate. Esther, as a nonpracticing Jew, warned my clergy husband, "Just don't say anything religious!" She asked me to sit with her at the service, inserting me between herself and her daughter. I kept busy passing tissues up and down the row while trying to console her as she howled. She did not hold back. She felt no embarrassment; her barrage of tears was her normal response to grief.

Several months after our son died, I realized that I had to make a decision. Was I going to be forever sad and become a diminished person because of his death, or would I choose to become an enlightened and better person? I made a conscious decision to use this tragedy to grow and become a better person because that is what our son would want. Have my tears stopped? No. They come now as a tribute to the past and as a welcome relief in the present.

What is it about tears that makes them so powerful—the release of water from our eyes, the sniffing of our noses, and the pinch in our throats? Tears are a physical reaction to our emotions and often to the pain in our hearts. Tears also appear when we're embarrassed or, surprisingly, feeling great joy. We can be moved to tears by kindness or by disappointment. How is it that our bodily response to seemingly opposite emotions is the same?

My father was not a crier, at least not in my presence. However, at the funeral service for his mother, I saw his shoulders shake and his hands reach to his eyes, and soft sobbing sounds came from his strong body. As he approached eighty, tears more easily slipped from his aged eyes. He told the story of his grandmother and how after her cow gave birth to a calf, she caressed the cow and spoke gentle words to her. The memory of her compassion moved him to tears.

I notice that men in our culture have more freedom to show anger than tears. Therefore, when tears would be the appropriate reaction to something, men may show anger. Joe, my brother-in-law, was only seven when his father died. He remembers holding back tears because he said to himself, "Big boys don't cry." At age seven, anger was acceptable, but tears were not. More than twenty years later, Joe shed tears over the death of our son, his nephew, but also, belatedly, over the death of his father. As my male relatives age, their tears come more easily, often unexpectedly. They appear to be surprised, sometimes embarrassed. Perhaps they feel out of control.

Conversely, since women have more freedom to shed tears, a woman may say, "I'll feel better after a good cry." My niece said, after the sudden death of her seventeen-year-old son, "I will cry for the rest of my life." I believe her. Tears will ease her sorrow and release tension. A wonderful Hebrew saying is "To remember is to bring back again." As my niece remembers her son, she will cry. The love she feels for her son comes out in tears because he is no longer physically present to receive her lavish love.

Unfortunately, some people feel that tears are unnecessary, saying "It's no use to cry over spilt milk" and "What's done is done." They urge a person to "buck up" as though tears are useless. As some tears dribble off my cheeks, I realize that tears are natural. They start at birth; we cry before we speak. The truth is tears are a gift.

# 4. HOME

WHEN GEORGE WAS IN assisted living recovering from his broken hip, his greeting each day as I entered his room was "I want to go home." Our young daughter on the first day of school also pleaded, "I want to go home." Our daughter yearned for home when she was in the dawn of life, my husband in the sunset.

Home is referred to as "my nest" or "a roof over my head" or "my personal doorway." Kahlil Gibran's definition, "Your house is your larger body," gives insight as to the personal nature of home, helping me understand why visitors say, "Your home looks like you." Whether our residence is palatial or modest, for most of us there is no place like home. Humans and animals have an innate desire for shelter, a place of protection. Our home shields us from severe weather, hateful people, and anything or anyone else harmful. It offers us privacy and a place to contemplate, welcoming us to put ourselves back in order after the whirlwind of some days.

A friend recently said, "The thing that makes me happy at this time of life is my little apartment. I like to socialize, to be involved in a variety of activities, but I am so happy that I can go home." I agree with him. One step through my doorway and I relax with a sigh of relief felt in my body and heard from my lips. My mind releases intensities, and my spirit does a little dance of freedom.

I can't imagine the pain and fear that people, young or old, experience if their home is not a shelter but rather a place where the body or spirit is harmed. How appalling, egregious, and evil it is to take from someone the sweetness of home as a haven of protection.

The idea of home also conjures places other than my own: my parents' home, our children's homes, even your home. We say, "I feel at home here," wherever *here* may be. Home is good; it's comfortable, it holds me, and I feel safe in it.

I discovered another kind of home as I learned about Alzheimer's disease. Until then I hadn't considered one's occupation as home. A study was undertaken where Alzheimer's patients had opportunities similar to their former employment. For example, a former custodian was given a "job" in the facility where he lived and received care for Alzheimer's. He swept the halls, locked doors and windows in the evening, turned off lights, and performed other tasks. A jumble of keys hung from his belt as a symbol of his importance. His memory didn't get better, but his sense of self-worth and his attitude improved markedly. He was once again home in his profession, which was a place of security for him.

An Alzheimer's patient may not be able to actually perform the duties of his or her former work, but it might be encouraging just to be able to talk about it. George was a theologian. I noticed that he was most comfortable—and at home, if you will—talking about theology. His interest or intent was not to convert but to discuss, explore, and question. He thrived on hearing diverse viewpoints. At this stage of Alzheimer's, he still had the ability to ponder, offer opinions, and ask questions. After sixty years of thinking and breathing theology, why would he—in fact, how could he—do otherwise?

People can engage us as we age by inquiring about our life's work, our second homes. We like to pontificate on what we did, learned, liked, disliked, miss, and don't miss. Whether our work was as a custodian for a business, a housekeeper in our own home, a CFO at a university, or our own budgeter, we have many stories to share that may increase our sense of worth and happiness.

The magic thing about home is that it feels good to leave, and it feels even better to come back. Can this be applied to our work homes as well? We're glad—some are thrilled—to be retired, but it feels good to go back, even if it is only in our dreams—or in our conversations.

# 5. VULNERABLE

WITH GEORGE CHANGING IN appearance and personality, I had a mission. I carried an envelope with its precious contents into the local OfficeMax. The clerk was busy but looked up and said, "You'll have to wait. I have three customers before you." Her tone was brisk, a bit snippy. She was probably thinking, "Why doesn't Jim—or somebody—come and help me?"

Finally, it was my turn. "Yes," Ms. Snippy said, "I can copy and enlarge your photo. Yes, it will be in color. Yes, it will be on glossy paper." She sighed at the same old dumb questions, took the photo, and clomped over to the machine. Her attitude said, "Why doesn't this woman use the self-help machine? Old people just don't get it."

Ms. Snippy returned with my copied photo in hand. My eyes lingered on it. I looked up, smiled, and said, "Perfect." Ms. Not-So-Snippy now was pleased that her customer was satisfied. "Who is that?" she asked. She raised her sculptured eyebrows and pointed to the photo.

"My husband," I responded. I didn't tell her, but looking at the photo I was reminded of his reddish-blond hair and his neatly trimmed beard. Here was the man who loved to tease but didn't smile or laugh easily. However, when he was greatly amused, he had a rollicking, throw-your-head-back, crinkled-eyes laugh.

She squinted to get a better look and said, "He looks young."

"Yes, that's him forty years ago. I want to hang it in our bedroom. He has Alzheimer's now. He needs to see himself as he used to be. And," a kink appeared in my throat, "I need the picture to remind me of the man I fell in love with."

This snippy young clerk—a stranger—came out from behind the counter. She came close, reached out, and surprised me with a generous hug.

"How kind you are," I whispered as I felt her strong child-woman arms around me. I gently pulled back and asked, "What do I owe you for the photo?"

She shook her head and said, "Nothing. My name is Jessie. I'm your new friend."

Wonder of wonders. Why did this brief exchange fill me with gratitude of greater proportions than one would guess? Kindness is always appreciated, but when we are vulnerable—hurt, frightened, ill, or just trying to make ends meet—the smallest positive intervention has great power. It can give someone a boost and the energy needed to carry on.

Unfortunately, when we are vulnerable, the smallest negative intervention is powerful as well. When our fifteen-year-old son died, a friend who took the Bible literally, including the verse "Rejoice always. Give thanks in all circumstances," said to me, "You should praise God for Todd's illness and death." Give me a break! I have never forgotten her words.

We long remember situations when someone said or did something negative or that we perceived as negative. We remember the time when a medical professional had poor bedside manners; the blunt, sharply expressed criticism from others; and the mean things someone said or did when we were children or teenagers. We carry these negatives like boulders in our memories. Do I believe that with God's help we can forgive and be released from such injury? Yes. But I want to honor the significance of positive and negative interventions. I ask myself, How many rock piles have I left in another's head?

I agree with a saying I heard recently: Be kind to those you meet; you never know what they might be going through. When we are vulnerable, the strength of that positive or negative is humongous. We don't forget. Thinking back on Jessie's small act of kindness, I realize it remains big in my mind. I know it's big because I even remember her name.

# 6. A TRAIN TRIP

IN MY DREAM I was on one of those express trains whizzing across the countryside so fast that my view from the window blurred. I wanted to get off. I pressed buttons, pounded on doors, and shouted at the conductor, but nothing worked. There was no way to get off the train. My heart hammered with fear; I could not leave.

When I awoke, my heart still reminded me of the dream's presence: bam, bam, bam, like a persistent carpenter with the steady beat of hammer on nail. I had never been much of a dream recorder or analyzer, but this one spoke to me. I was on a journey on the Alzheimer's train as I cared for my beloved husband diagnosed with this disease. The dream told me that even as I wanted to care for him, a hidden, subconscious part of me was frightened and wanted to get off the train.

I appreciated many things about George. Lately, I was so appreciative that he acknowledged his diagnosis of Alzheimer's. He reminded me to inform people and even suggested that I share my writings. Such transparency made it easier for me. There was no denial or uncomfortable hush-hush. He readily said in conversation, "I can't see. I can't hear. And I can't remember." Such a forthright approach put everyone at ease.

As the disease progressed, the big looming question was, How will we (I) manage? I had four priorities.

My first priority was to keep George safe. Some days I tired of hearing my own voice: "Use your walker. The seat on the walker is helpful if you want to rest. Here's a glass of juice. Your pills are on the table. Our schedule for today is on the whiteboard on the refrigerator. Wear your safety pendant." On and on.

I felt like I was becoming his mother. I worried that I was watching over him like a child. A wise friend reminded me, "Vivian, you are not his mother. You are his memory." What amazing insight! Her simple statement put my caregiving into perspective. I was his memory.

My second priority was to provide stimulation for George: mental, emotional, and spiritual. Since his sight and hearing were diminished, it was important to help him see and hear. He enjoyed listening to books on his Kindle, a gift from our daughters and their husbands. He used a lighted and magnified reading device to read some material. One routine we both enjoyed took place at the morning breakfast table: I read emails and Facebook posts to him. That way he was aware of the news of family and friends. I was also a big photo-album maker. George remembered trips and events as he scanned the old albums, asking me to read the captions.

Later in the day, I read our mail to him. It was a gift when a personal letter or card poked out from the pile of advertisements. When he heard the kind words written to and about him, he perked up and his eyes danced (not like a polka, more like a waltz). One of George's favorite activities was patio time. He settled into his comfortable chair, pillow behind his back and feet resting on a footstool, and thought. Wearing his ever-present Norwegian sea captain's hat, he waved and nodded to those who passed by. With diminished sight and hearing, he didn't always recognize the people but greeted them nevertheless. The sun warmed his body, and the patio experience warmed his soul.

My third priority was to involve others in his well-being. Fortunately, we had several families: our immediate and extended family, the church family, our worldwide friends, and the family here at Regents Point, a continuing-care community. As a friend said, "Let me do something. It makes *me* feel better." George truly appreciated it when people came over and read to him. This provided both social and intellectual stimulation. I learned to invite people to accompany us on outings. Their company was of great help to me, and it gave George interaction with others besides his ever-present wife. We continued our long practice of inviting people for wine and cheese in our home. The presence of others provided a social life for both of us.

While much of my energy went into focusing on keeping George safe and stimulated and involving others in his well-being, I had a fourth priority: caring for myself. In our relationship, I valued him; however, as in any relationship, it was important to value myself as well. I learned the benefits of respite. Time away renewed my energy and desire to continue the dual role of caregiver and wife. It helped me maintain a lightness of spirit, affection, and humor—all the sweet parts of marriage.

In my most vulnerable times, I didn't know if I could manage. Like my train dream suggested, did I want to leave and get off the Alzheimer's train? Absolutely not. My resolve was as firm and deep as the roots of the three-hundred-year-old tree that I admired in the park. I didn't want to get off the Alzheimer's train; I wanted to learn to ride it. This was important for me to underscore to George. I didn't want him to worry that I would leave—physically or emotionally. I would not abandon him. I would love him.

At the conclusion of the communion service at our church, we always say these words that never fail to bring tears to my eyes: "Give thanks always and everywhere that life is precious beyond all telling."

Yes, life is precious beyond all telling, even with Alzheimer's.

# 7. THE LAST PICTURE SHOW

"WOULD YOU LIKE TO go to a movie today?" I asked George, hoping for a fun outing.

"I guess so. Which one?"

"*Harriet.* I've heard that it's very good."

"Who's Harriet?"

"Harriet Tubman. She helped her family and many other people out of slavery."

"Oh. Okay."

Off we went. George didn't want to use his walker, choosing his cane instead. I dropped him off in front of the theater and requested that he wait for me to assist him up the stairs. I parked the car and returned to George. He wasn't there. I ran around and finally found him in the lobby sitting comfortably in a green chair. "Honey, I wish you would have waited for me. I worry that you might fall."

"Oh," he said with nonchalance.

I left to buy our tickets and get a hearing device for him to wear over his hearing aids: they were clumsy headphones with a contraption about the size of two decks of cards. "Let's go find the right theater," I said to George when I got back over to him.

He wasn't ready to go. "I want some popcorn."

Off I went, this time for popcorn. I returned to George, helped him get up, and, with the popcorn in one hand, the hearing device in the other, and George holding on to my shoulder with one hand and the cane in his other, we shuffled toward the correct theater. It was a balancing act.

"I need a bottle of water," George said. Neither of us had a third hand.

"Sorry, George, we can't get water." I used my authoritative voice. He grumbled under his breath.

The theater lights were off and previews were on the screen. With baby steps we searched for our assigned seats (a new wrinkle concocted by the theater), and after stumbling into and out of incorrect rows, George refused to go any further. I coaxed him to sit relatively near our assigned spot.

We settled in, George chomped on the popcorn, the headphones were in place, and the main feature was soon to begin. Now I could relax.

"These things don't work," George said as he yanked the headphones off and plopped them in my lap. I tried them and I could hear just fine. He tried again. Off they came. I juggled them on my lap along with his cane.

The movie started. "One of my hearing aids needs a new battery. I can't find the battery bag." Oh great! I reached over and checked his pockets. Nope. Better check the floor. As distasteful as it was, I kneeled down and scuttled my hands across the sticky floor. Found it.

"I can't get the battery in. Can you do it?" he said. I took the hearing aid and the teeny-weeny battery. In the pitch-dark theater, I tried to join them. It wasn't easy, but I eventually did it. Happy day. George was set: he had his hearing aids and popcorn. He could sit back and enjoy the show.

Wrong. The questions started.

"Which one is Harriet?" he asked in his be-sure-they-can-hear-you voice.

"Who is that?"

"Are they married?"

"I can't see them. What are they doing?"

"What did she say?"

Our running dialogue continued throughout the show, with me shushing him and trying to answer his questions with elevated whispers into his hearing aid. I felt bad that he had such difficulties, but I must admit that it was a relief when the movie ended. We got up, gathered our stuff, crunched our way over dropped popcorn, and stumbled and bumbled to the aisle. By the time we made it to the car, I was worn out.

"What did you think about the movie?" I asked.

"It was good, but I couldn't hear or see very well."

The next day he told everyone we met, *"Harriet* is a great movie. You should see it."

I nodded and with an inaudible sigh told myself that it was the last picture show I'd take him to. Ever.

# 8. SPACE

AS I OPENED THE door of the hotel room, I felt a catch in my throat and wetness on my cheeks. Tears burst forth like they were finally escaping a great holding place behind my eyeballs. The tears came as awareness dawned on me: I have this clean, quiet, lovely room all to myself for two full days. The feeling of relief, I admitted to myself, turned on the faucet of tears.

I was there because George said, "I've got an idea. I think you should go away for a couple days, have some time to yourself." I suspected that my recent diagnosis of hives and rash precipitated this thought. Whatever the genesis, the suggestion was appreciated.

But I still debated. Should I, could I? I hesitated, though not for long.

My response was similar to that of being asked, "Would you like some ice cream?" One day later, I had a hotel reservation and made arrangements with our daughter to provide care for George.

People and articles told me that caregivers need time away. My friends said, "Be sure to take care of yourself,

Vivian." My daughters cautioned, "Mom, you need some time away." Members of my support group were equally compassionate: "How are you holding up? Plan time for yourself." I've said the same thing to others.

So, here I was in a hotel doing just that. My unexpected tears told me a truth so deeply hidden that I didn't allow it to surface: I *needed* this escape.

Of course, I loved my husband, and I wanted to help care for him. He was frail and needed me. But, if truth be told, caregiving is not easy. Caring for an adult's daily needs is a lot of hard work—making sure that correct medications are given at the correct time, cleaning up after toileting and upset stomach, doing laundry, paying bills, and preparing income taxes, all with constant sleep-interrupted nights. Plus I was chauffeur and a listening ear at sixteen medical appointments in eight weeks. (Lest you think I exaggerate, I counted.) No matter how much one wants to help, no matter how appreciative the receiver is, caregiving is not easy.

On the other hand, it's not easy to let go, take time away, and retreat. Even though this focus on myself was temporary, it felt selfish, as if I was neglecting my duty. Then, I read the wise words of writer Henri Nouwen: "A life . . . without a quiet center, becomes destructive." So in my hotel room I read, wrote, reflected, napped, and ate when and what I wanted. Best of all, I was quiet.

Two days later the time had come to return home. I was ready. Just as the space key is important in typing, we need space in life. The last two days were my space keys that allowed me to relax, analyze, and bring clarity to my life. Not only is space important, it's imperative. Once again, words from Henri Nouwen rested in my heart: "Whenever we . . . spend quiet time away from the places where we interact with each other directly, we are potentially opened for a deeper intimacy with each other."

Home I went. I felt restored, invigorated, and refreshed. I kissed George, then I had some ice cream.

# *9.* WHAT ARE YOU DOING?

ONE MORNING, WE DECIDED to go for a pleasant morning outing to the local Dunkin' Donuts. We invited our friend Susie to join us. When she arrived at our door, I called, "George, it's time to leave." He came out to the living room, looking cute in his khaki shorts and pressed plaid shirt, all ready to go—except he was carrying a urinal. (Not exactly the fashion statement you want to make.) I exchanged glances with our friend, whose eyebrows had jumped to her hairline. I suggested that he leave the urinal at home. George did not agree. After a bit of coaxing, he let me place the urinal in a cloth bag to accompany us on our way. Fortunately, it was not pulled out and used at Dunkin' Donuts.

Later, as we arrived home, a voice from the backseat said, "Don't tell Susie, but I just peed in the urinal." I glanced at our friend; her astonished face and wide eyes told it all. I wondered again, Who are you and what *are* you doing?

A couple weeks later, George took a drinking glass from a fancy restaurant. We learned of it when we got into our daughter's car. "Where did you get that, Dad?"

"Oh," he responded. "I took it. I might need it to go to the bathroom on my way home."

"Not in my car," she said.

Despite the changes in George, he usually remained a gentle, kind person. He sometimes said, "You are wonderful. You help me so much." I cherish those words. Sitting at the table at a family birthday celebration with our daughters and their husbands, George said, "I have something to say." His blue eyes were intense. "When I die," he paused as tears escaped from that sea of blue, "be sure to take care of your mother." His words were squeezed out like they were coming from underwater. "She is so good to me." Now all our eyes were wet.

# *10.* HOPE

I MISSED SOME ASPECTS of George from our younger years.

I missed George's physical strength, like his ability to forcefully hit a tennis or golf ball, lift heavy items, or open impossible-to-get-into packages.

I missed his ability to drive, his willingness to spend hours behind the wheel.

I missed his keen hearing. I could no longer whisper to him in the theater, at church, or even snug in bed in the quiet of the night.

I missed his sharp eyesight and his voracious reading.

I missed sharing memories from our almost-a-lifetime together as his recall diminished.

I missed how he entered a room and took over. After his diagnosis, he sat quietly in a chair, a smaller version of his former self, often missing much of the conversation.

I missed his hearty appetite: three square meals a day and, to top it off, ice cream at bedtime.

I missed hearing him say, "Guess what, honey," when he had news to share and we'd converse about our workday.

I missed the ease of intimacy when pain and fatigue didn't thwart desire.

The list goes on. I think about what else changes with time: I love a fragrant orange blossom; however, it fades. I love babies; they grow. I love a sunset; it disappears. Everything has its time of productivity, then fades with age. Do I love a tree less because it is old? No, there is beauty in its gnarled branches, thick bark, and bent limbs. However, eventually, the tree and everything else fades with age.

Instead of asking, What's missing? I learned to focus on the positive and ask, What is? Like the old tree, there is much to enjoy as we humans fade. Humor is one thing that is here. In fact, our losses often lead to humor. We laugh at our many foibles. We laugh at how often we misplace things, mistakenly wear our slippers out to dinner, and forget to put the carafe under the coffee maker, causing a flood of coffee. Poet Emily Dickinson wrote, "You cannot fold a flood / and put it in a drawer." One look in our cupboard drawer and you'll see that we proved her wrong. You get the point: there's plenty to give us a good laugh.

Another welcome addition is the ability and time to sit on the patio and watch the hijinks of the squirrels, birds, and butterflies. Patio time offers a superb pondering opportunity. George often came in from the patio and asked about things we had once done, leading us into conversation. Whether your quiet place is the patio, the kitchen table, or a rock in the park, it is wonderful to have the time to reflect.

One of my favorite things about "What is?" is the permission we have to set our own schedules and make our own choices. Well, we don't have complete control but certainly more than when we were young. If I want soup for breakfast, I have it. Nobody rebuked George for eating two cookies for his first meal of the day. I don't have to take that nasty cod liver oil of my youth, with people telling me, "You must swallow it, Vivian. It's good for you." I'd rather have my current cholesterol pill. And don't you love it that a nap can happen anytime and with any frequency?

"What are you up to on Saturday morning? Think I could stop by?" read the text on my iPhone. If I believed in the rapture, I would have asked God to hold off; a visit from a grandchild takes preeminence. Our grandson Andy, at twenty-three years of age, spent the morning with us, talking of his life and asking about ours. It was more difficult in our earlier years to take the time for a drop-everything visit. I like the what-is opportunities of being older.

An unknown author captures feelings of sorrow—the what's-missing outlook—mixed with feelings of hope:

> I believe in the sun, even when it is not shining.
> I believe in love, even when I am alone.
> I believe in God, even when God is silent.

These inspiring words were found inscribed on a basement wall written by someone hiding from the Gestapo during World War II. Later, the words were put to music by Michael Horvit. For this anonymous writer, the sun, love, and God were missing, yet he or she believed in them. The losses of aging certainly can't be compared to the horrors of war and the Holocaust, yet feelings of loss, no matter the reason, have some affinity despite their diversity of situation and degree. What I appreciate about this beautiful writing is the hope in the midst of loss that the author captures.

Things will not always be as they once were. Rather than responding with fear or anger, I want to hold on to hope.

# *11.* Zzz

GEORGE WAS SLEEPING, AT least I thought so. I looked more closely. Was his chest rhythmically moving, assuring me of his beating heart? I remembered studying our babies in this way while they slept. Now I did it once again as I watched my husband sleep. A mild form of panic arose in my body when he looked like he wasn't breathing. I took a closer look, then relaxed. His Alzheimer's plus severe kidney disease had put me in alert mode.

I'm thankful that we both slept quite well. Let me modify that statement. With Alzheimer's, my husband had acquired a bouncing movement during the night. He was completely unaware of, and unable to control, the bouncing of his legs and arms. I learned to adapt, but sometimes I moved to the couch. George slept well despite visiting that little room with the nightlight next to our bedroom numerous times during the night. Each morning, as we made the bed, I loved the warmth of the bedding on the side where he slept. Would there be a morning when my hands touched cool sheets?

When I was a little girl, a picture hung on my bedroom wall. It portrayed a girl—like me—kneeling at her bedside. The words of her prayer were inscribed below her:

Now I lay me down to sleep.
I pray the Lord my soul to keep.
If I should die before I wake,
I pray the Lord my soul to take.

*"If I should die before I wake"*—I don't recall that phrase conjuring up fear in my little blonde head. Perhaps I recited it by rote with no thought of its meaning. One would think that those words could have been scary to a child. Now, at this stage of life, I hear many older people say that they hope they die in their sleep. They perceive that as a great way to go.

Something extraordinary happens as you age when it comes to sleep. I used to wonder how anyone could fall asleep in a chair an hour after getting up from a good night's rest. It happened to me one day. Warm coffee, buttered toast with apricot jam, a cozy shawl, and my black leather lounge chair all wooed me back into slumber at eight o'clock in the morning. It felt great!

And then there's the afternoon nap, my favorite. I've treated myself to a nap most days since I retired twenty years ago. One year, we celebrated our wedding anniversary with brunch at Lulu's cafe, a French restaurant.

Home again, I was feeling full, content, and drowsy, so I lay down for a nap. When I awoke, I couldn't open the bedroom door. The handle was missing. No matter what I tried, the door wouldn't open.

I called, "Yoo-hoo, George." Louder, "George!" No response. Using my cell phone, I called the landline. No response either. I could hear George in the house, but he didn't hear me, nor the phone, because of his diminished hearing. "Yoo-hoo, George!" Eventually, the house grew quiet.

Unbeknownst to me, while I slept George came in and removed the door handle, which needed repairing. I later learned that he went to Home Depot with the broken door handle. This was surprising because George is not Mr. Fix-It.

Two whole hours later, George opened the bedroom door. "Time to fix wine and cheese, Vivian."

I'm probably not the first anniversary celebrant to spend two hours locked in a bedroom. But I'm probably the only one who did so while alone. It was almost enough to make a preacher's wife swear.

In the evening, we liked to retire earlier than we once did. One night a couple of years ago, we were all cozy and in that twilight zone before falling asleep. The telephone rang. George reached over and picked up the receiver With nary a hello, he asked, "What are you thinking, calling us at this late hour?" His tone was less than pleasant, a tad bit scolding. I looked at the clock. It was 8:30.

Though the telephone was sometimes the culprit for interrupted sleep, some nights I tossed and turned, not understanding why sleep eluded us. It was then that I experienced the world at its worst. Everything was worrisome, including my own life. In the darkness of the night, I feared I might become ill and not be able to care for George. I related to the words that Henry Kissinger is rumored to have said: "There cannot be a crisis next week. My schedule is already full." It is as though dark thoughts arise to match the darkness of the night. In the light of a new day, a spirit of lightness returns.

Recently, my husband had begun a new practice: he gently rubbed my back, helping to quiet my body and soul and lead me into sleep. It was one of the sweetest things he could have done for me. I loved it. In that comfortable zone, I mused that someday the breath of life will leave us. When that happens, our sleep—whether morning, noon, or night—will surely be peaceful. If we believe in heaven or not, we will sleep in heavenly peace.

# *12.* CREATIVE COPING

ONE OF MY CONCERNS was how we would manage as George's memory and health decreased. I was well aware that part of the answer was that I needed to take care of myself. I didn't want to feel put-upon, resentful, or worn thin like a used rug. I didn't want to feel like I was in a deep, dark hole. I wanted to feel whole. This is not just a play on words—from *hole* to *whole*; it was a necessity. In my professional life I worked with people in bereavement stemming from loss: loss over a death, divorce, job, illness, or relationship to name a few. They taught me the following creative coping strategies.

- *Savor*—Rediscover the senses of sight, sound, touch, smell, and taste. See the beauty of a flower, smell an orange, listen to your favorite music, eat popcorn, or stroke a pet. I learned that sometimes I needed to buy something for my soul. My soul needed flowers, so I spent eight dollars on a Trader Joe's floral bouquet. That didn't blow our budget. Rather, flowers paid dividends because they were soothing, like medicine on an abrasion, a salve to the soul. Lady Bird Johnson said it well: "Where flowers bloom, so does hope." It is important for our spirits to savor the present.

- *Express yourself verbally*—A Danish proverb states, "Shared sorrow is half sorrow." Verbal expression may be one on one, as with a friend, clergyperson, or professional counselor, or with several people, as in a small support group. It is important to feel safe by knowing that our listeners are trustworthy and our words will be kept confidential.

- *Express yourself physically*—Write, paint, build, sew, sing, dance, or play an instrument. Such activities calm us and help put things into perspective. Or if we're angry, we may get great satisfaction out of attacking weeds, hitting balls, or pounding nails. Jabbing at inanimate objects is preferred to jabbing people. Athletic endeavors like walking or exercising can relieve tension and depression. Laughing and crying, as well as touching tenderly, certainly ease tension. All of these are forms of physical expression.

- *Ask for help*—I've learned the importance of asking for support. My family, plus a social worker and chaplain, convinced me (finally) to hire a caregiver to assist with George's care. While I was learning to ask for help, it was especially gratifying when a friend or family member took the initiative and offered help. Our granddaughter called and offered to run errands for me. A friend had some photos enlarged so George's dim eyes could see them. Another washed my car.

- *Develop a spirit of wonder*—Plan for spaces in your schedule to pause. For me, wonder emerges when I contemplate the extravagantly beautiful Australian willow tree in our front yard. Its chunky bark and expansive arms open my soul to a feeling of awe. That, in turn, leads me to a spiritual dimension that brings gratitude, perspective, and hope. A sense of wonder can release energy that was tied up in guilt, self-pity, hatred, or just plain fatigue. For some, another word for wonder is *worship*, a sacred time for listening to God and allowing contentment and peace to seep into one's core.

- *Explore*—Information seeking is exciting and helps us handle the anxiety of facing the unfamiliar. Plus new knowledge broadens our self-esteem. I like to look up medical information and medications on the Mayo Clinic website. A friend of mine is prone to depression. To cope, she explores other people's lives by a phone call, email, or snail mail. That way, she gets new ideas and builds on the creativity of others.

- *Find balance*—To be whole, we need balance between solitude and social life. We are social creatures. Being with people we enjoy is so satisfying;

we draw strength from them and are energized in their presence. However, whether we are extroverts or introverts, times of solitude are also important. Author Christina Baldwin claims that silence provides direction. Silence is a source of insight that guides us in knowing what to do or not do.

- *Nibble*—When life seems overwhelming, it is helpful to group tasks or problems into manageable pieces. Then we can nibble at them, completing or solving a few at a time. Sometimes we feel guilty or powerless in the face of so many needs. While we may be unable to change the situation, our nibbles can aid our feeling of accomplishment.
- *Set goals*—We all need something to look forward to. It need not be large in scope: it may be the goal of rewarding yourself with tea and cookies at the end of a long day. It could be as lavish as planning a trip.

Author Sue Monk Kidd describes the soul as the rich, inner life of the psyche where the deepest impulse is to create wholeness. That's what I desire. I want to be whole—yes, even in the midst of loss. As we face inevitable loss in our lives, may we be wise enough to practice positive, creative coping strategies.

# 13. THE BOOK

I WATCHED AND LISTENED as George carried on a deep conversation reminiscing about the past. I thought, He's his old self. Maybe he doesn't have Alzheimer's. Maybe it's like when I get the sniffles, sneeze a bit, and presume that I'm coming down with a cold only to discover it was just a day of sniffles and sneezing, nothing more.

This shows the ambivalence found in living with someone with dementia. Friends said, "George is the same. I don't see anything different." They implied "Are you sure that the diagnosis is correct?" I asked myself, Is it really true?

In wrestling with the diagnosis, I learned to celebrate George's conversations and actions those "normal" days. I needed to celebrate because the next day or hour could be different. Then I was reminded that it was true. It was as though the Alzheimer's brain said, "I think I'll use my good cells today. Tomorrow, maybe not." At this stage of Alzheimer's, most of the negative manifestations are hidden from the public; I experienced them in private.

On my birthday, I was up early savoring a couple of hours of quiet time before George awoke. (This in itself was different; he used to always be up early and at his office by 7:30.) While sipping a cup of café au lait and nibbling on a chocolate croissant (a birthday treat), I opened my emails. My Minnesota friend Sharon wrote, "On your birthday, do you think about the past year or the year ahead?" Sharon, my junior by twenty years, often raised questions for me to contemplate.

I think I looked at both the past and future. First, the past year. That's easy: the Alzheimer's diagnosis took priority over everything. Though unwelcome, it gave an explanation to what I was observing and experiencing. It provided clarity, just as the early morning coastal fog dissipates and provides a glimpse of clear sky.

Looking ahead, yes, I would love and care for George. But what about my own life? I remembered the paper chains we made in elementary school, link after colorful link. In marriage we were like three links: one for George's independent life, one for my independent life, and a joining link signifying our lives together. The center link was our marriage, but we each retained the essence of self. With an Alzheimer's diagnosis, it felt like the center link was the only link, the one that took precedence. Would there be any me, or would I be swallowed by us?

For example, George, in his infinite desire to contribute to the lives of others, decided to put together what he called "his last book." I had concerns due to his diminished sight and hearing as well as his Alzheimer's diagnosis. We conferred with our daughters and their husbands and, while applauding his idea, they cautioned that I should not take on more responsibility as my hands were already full. A friend offered to help, so we finally decided to go ahead. A contract was signed with an editor.

Helen Keller is known to have said, "The only thing worse than being blind is having sight but no vision." Our family was united in pride over George's vision to continue to make a contribution, this time by compiling articles by a variety of writers related to the title *Silence Is Not the Answer*. George's intent was to bring the book out soon so it could offer an intellectual and informed approach to presidential and other elections. He believed that thoughtful people needed to speak out on important justice issues rather than remain silent for fear of being misunderstood or ostracized.

I thought George needed this project. I was well aware that it would require my help—I wanted to help—yet I remained apprehensive. What if his health deteriorated? How about more memory loss? Could he complete the responsibilities required in the contract? If not, who would? In spite of my family's cautions, I knew I would be involved.

Oh, the ambivalence! I wanted to be upbeat yet clear-eyed. Would the work on the book allow me the luxury of living my life in addition to fulfilling this commitment to my husband? Was my paper chain link, the independent one, still viable?

I decided that I was overthinking this. Where was my self-described positive thinking? I needed to trust the process. While I served as George's eyes, ears, and memory, his creative capacity still yearned to express itself. I recalled Beethoven, a composer of the eighteenth and nineteenth centuries that we admire to this day. By his late twenties, his hearing began to deteriorate. When he was almost totally deaf, he composed his greatest works. Think of that! What a tragedy it would have been if someone had told him he was no longer capable of creative expression. George needed this project, and I would help.

An analogy came to mind: The path before me is unknown and dark, black as a moonless night. But motion lights surprise me, illuminating the path with each step I take. I wanted this picture to sustain me in my ambivalence. I would take a step, light would appear, another step, light would appear again, and forward I would go, one step at a time.

# *14.* CONNECTIONS

GEORGE HAD ANOTHER HOSPITALIZATION due to a urinary tract infection that went into his kidneys. Once again, he went into assisted living after the hospital discharged him. He had been there about a week when I walked into his room. He was visibly upset.

His soft blue eyes hardened as he said, "Do you realize how disappointed you make me?" His words stung. "Do you realize how sad you make me?" Ouch. "You didn't come to see me right when you got home."

I was stunned. I had just returned from a three-day trip with our daughters, a needed respite from caregiving. The night before I left, I was distraught over my husband's disconcerting comments to two young visitors. I was glad to get away. When we returned, our daughters went straight to visit their dad so I could take a nap before spending the evening with him.

I attempted to redirect his negative comments: "I'm sorry you're upset, honey. Did you enjoy the afternoon with our daughters? I needed a nap, but now I'm here to have dinner and spend the evening with you."

My explanation didn't satisfy him. He remained glum throughout dinner and the evening. Was this the same man who urged me to take time away to care for myself and the kind man who cared about the suffering people of the world? Yes, this was that same man but with a new voice, the voice of Alzheimer's. Perhaps he was distraught because he perceived me as his anchor and his connection to the world.

I sensed a growing disconnect and detachment as his Alzheimer's brain changed. I watched as he disconnected from his body. Once a tennis and golf enthusiast with good body coordination, he now was unbalanced and walked with a shuffle. Occasionally, he tried to correct that but soon returned to the walk with which he was comfortable. He was slow, only as fast as his elderly limbs could carry him. He no longer attended the morning exercise classes he used to enjoy three times a week.

Another disconnect I noticed was a detachment from people, conversations, and activities; I saw a shrinking within himself—not always, but often. While part of his disconnect was likely due to his diminished sight and hearing, it appeared that his interest in people and his motivation to connect had changed. He rarely used the skills he was taught to help him hear, such as leaning forward and looking at people to read their lips.

He also began to disconnect with the past. I learned to avoid saying, "Do you remember . . ." Instead, I chose an event, recalled the details, then concluded with something like, "You enjoyed that so much." He liked to hear about the activity, even if he couldn't recall it. On our way to gatherings of family or friends, we went over the names of attendees. He liked to review places and events as though attempting to hold on to them. In reviewing his life story, was he hanging on to his existence? Was he authenticating his life?

His frustration increased when attempting to use technology. I could relate to that. However, his disconnect with it was greater than that experienced by many of the elderly. My help was essential, and believe you me, I am not an expert! Numerous times, when he was seated in front of the desktop computer, I heard, "Vivian! Come here. Find my email. Make the print larger. How do you send this? I can't find . . ." The same was true with his Kindle that he used to listen to books. I could explain a function, but it disappeared in the clouds of his Alzheimer's brain.

George's clearest connection was with his lifelong profession. His dreams almost always centered around his work as a clergyperson. He continued to enjoy attending clergy meetings, talking about religion and politics, and wrestling with philosophical issues—sometimes to the consternation of others because they grew impatient and wanted to move on to other topics.

I grieved for him in his many disconnects. It appeared, however, that I was more distraught over these than he was. Perhaps Alzheimer's softened the emotional impact of his losses. He did recognize his losses and said, "You are lucky you can see, hear, and remember so well."

I looked for some positives: Alzheimer's isn't physically painful. My husband was in his mideighties, whereas many patients are much younger. Our family was fully aware of our situation, with no denials, and unselfishly gave love and care to both of us. We lived in a continuing-care community where people were understanding and supportive. He retained the ability to carry on a conversation. He was grateful for my help—not always, but mostly. We continued to have a connection. I had some me-time while he slept.

My beloved had a fading memory, his eyes and ears grew dim, and his limbs were weak. Yet there was something for which to be grateful: he still recognized my face.

# *15.* HALLELUJAH!

THE HOUSE WAS QUIET. My man sat on the patio silently. The refrigerator's funky gurgles were the sole sounds that accompanied a glorious exploding in my brain—the words "Hallelujah, hallelujah, hallelujah!" George's book had gone to press. He did it. We did it. George was happy; I was happily relieved.

I think George relished the opportunity that the book provided to make important decisions once again. Therefore, he struggled with the editor and me when we disagreed with some of his decisions. We attempted to be accommodating; after all, it *was* his book. However, the editor's experience provided the knowledge to put a book together. We needed to listen.

I was the bridge between the editor and George, relaying messages back and forth. The editor referred to George as "my favorite troublemaker." Despite Alzheimer's, George frequently came up with good thoughts and ideas. Other times, both the editor and I just couldn't go along with his suggestions. George had a strong personality, so those times were dicey. I'm not proud of myself when in my frustration, I occasionally lost my temper. I reminded myself, "Vivian, cool it. Back off. Let the decision rest overnight." Sometimes that worked; George would be more amenable to the editor's suggestion the next day.

When the book finally got into the printer's hands, I felt such a relief! When the book was ready, we'd move on to the marketing phase. That would hopefully be less stressful. I kept my fingers (and toes) crossed.

Something had dawned on me: I was content in my marriage. It had taken me a long time to understand some aspects of it. I learned that an intimate relationship involved what psychologists refer to as love and hate in the marriage state. They claim that even the happiest marriages include the harboring of some hostile feelings. Though *hate* is a strong word for me—I am more comfortable with *dislike*—the truth is that we encounter such opposites as love and hate in our closest relationships. I wasn't able to admit that to myself until now. I saw negative feelings as failure on my part or my husband's. When I disliked him, I felt guilty and attempted to dismiss ithe feeling as unreasonable, or I'd swallow my dislike and pretend it wasn't so. After all, didn't I promise to love him till death? I was learning that having times of dislike was normal; it doesn't mean that love was missing. Our emotions ran the spectrum between the strong poles of love and hate. I no longer had to fear the negativity I felt at times. I could let it sit with me, stew in its juices, and not feel the relationship was falling apart. I didn't have to feel like I was in love every day of our married lives.

The second major insight I had was that I didn't fully understand my husband's reason for putting his work first in his life. Neurosurgeon Paul Kalanithi writes in his book, *When Breath Becomes Air* (Random House, 2016), that when graduating from medical school, he and the other students worked on writing their commencement oath. He recalls, "Several students argued for the removal of language insisting that we place our patients' interests above our own. . . . This kind of egotism struck me as antithetical to medicine and, it should be noted, entirely reasonable. Indeed, this is how 99 percent of people select their jobs: pay, work environment, hours. But that's the point. Putting lifestyle first is how you find a job—not a calling."

That was how George lived his life. To him, his work had been a calling. As admirable as this may have been, such a belief held some negatives. When work comes first, one's family may suffer even if they understand and accept the premise of a calling. I now understood why George worked as he did, yet it didn't take away the occasional yearnings I had for it to be different. His success, however, was directly related to his willingness to take on the mantle of his calling.

So, the question now is, Is my contentment today partly based on my having more control of my life rather than living according to George's schedule and his always calling the shots? Somehow, I experienced a new independence even while caring for George remained at the center of my attention. I was more my own person. His strong will remained but was now tempered by the disabilities of his aging. Even with Alzheimer's he seemed to more clearly notice and appreciate me on a deeper level, including my work ethic, talents, and presence. While in the past we were focused on his life, now he paid more attention to me as a person, someone separate from himself. I was content.

# *16.* STRUGGLE

WE PLANNED TEN CELEBRATIONS to launch the book here in California. It also was decided that I would go to Minnesota, our former stomping grounds, as George's ambassador to introduce the book. Two book events would be held in the Minneapolis–St. Paul area. It was settled.

Then a week later, George said, his eyes strong with conviction, "I've decided that I want to go to Minnesota with you to launch the book. Think about it, Vivian. Don't answer yet."

My stomach clenched. How would he manage a trip in his frail condition? Travel was tough. Germs of all sorts were shared on a plane. Then where would he get the energy for a book signing, talking, and shaking hands? And how would I manage taking care of him plus keeping track of all the details of a book launch two thousand miles from home?

Knowing that arguing didn't work, I said, "Hmm, let's think about it."

The next day George had an appointment with the nephrologist, his kidney doctor. I took this opportunity to run the Minnesota idea past him. With his dark eyes locked on George and a hand gently touching his arm, the doctor said, "No. I cannot condone that. Even I, a much younger person, find that travel is difficult on my body. You would end up in the hospital away from home." My stomach unclenched.

George excused himself to use the restroom. The nephrologist said to me, "He is very frail. Death is not imminent, but . . ." Thank God for this supportive, compassionate truth teller.

When we returned home, we sat at the kitchen table to review the appointment, as was our custom. George said, "Well, the doctor didn't say I can't go to Minnesota."

Oh brother! I attempted to remind him of the conversation: "Let me tell you what I heard the doctor say. He said, 'No, I can't condone that. I understand that you want to see Minnesota for the last time. It is an emotional need. I get that. But the medical aspect is what is important now. You are not able to travel, you would end up in the hospital, and I must not condone it.'"

After a few hours, George seemed to accept my recall of the doctor's decision. However, two days later he said, "I don't have to do what the doctor says."

I nodded and said, "But I'm so glad that you will."

That night when he lay in bed, I went to him and gave him his good-night hug and kiss. He looked at me with his still beautiful soft-blue eyes and murmured, "You are so good to me. I never tire of looking at you."

I smiled all night.

People asked me, "How was it to help George bring his new book to fruition?" I had two answers: it was both a struggle and an honor.

On the one hand, the process was difficult. George's health issues played a large part in that. Diminished hearing meant that I was the go-between with George and the editor on all the phone communications. Diminished sight meant that using the computer was too difficult for George, and all written communications had to be read to him. His severe kidney disease contributed to his low energy level. His hip replacement surgery impaired his walking ability. Finally, the Alzheimer's diagnosis added to the struggle.

However—and it was a big however—putting the book together was an honor. I had the opportunity to work with a knowledgeable and efficient editor, communicate with contributing authors, and obtain testimonies as to the importance of the book. George, with all his health issues, still had the will and conviction that he wanted to make a contribution. What a lesson that was to me: if George could do it, I and others could make contributions as well. We may think we are too small to make a difference, but an old saying applies here: if you think you're too small to make a difference, you've never been in bed with a mosquito. Thank you, George, for the opportunity to work on your book project. It was a struggle and an honor.

# *17.* HOLLY AND JOLLY

AS CHRISTMAS APPROACHED, I began to think about decorating our home, especially as I listened to the words on one of our CDs: "Deck the halls with boughs of holly, Fa, la, la, la, la, la, la, la, la."

Deck the halls! I've always enjoyed decorating for Christmas. But our situation was different now. With an apartment of 734 square feet, we did not have much space and certainly no halls in which to hang holly. Besides, would we have any guests to see them? Well, I decided, I'll put up a few decorations, George liked them, and in the future he may not have the same capacity to enjoy them due to his progressing dementia. I would do it for *him*.

The maintenance man, the personification of patience, dragged out the Christmas box from storage. I opened it. It emitted a musky odor from being tucked away in a dark cupboard for a year. What should I take out to put on the coffee table? I thought. There was the pure-white ceramic holy family, a gift from our wedding attendants, Bruce and Gloria. Memories floated out as I placed it in the center of the table. I saw the glass snowball candleholders that we purchased the year we lived in Sweden. More memories resurfaced as they graced the table. Joan gave me this shiny angel. Nan and Ian presented us with these elegant candleholders for our fiftieth wedding anniversary. With more memories coming up, I was having fun.

George gingerly entered the room, sat in his favorite chair with the worn armrests, and watched. I unwrapped the eucalyptus tree candleholders, a wedding gift from fifty-nine years ago. George asked about them with eyes that betrayed his lack of recall. They looked just right standing on the ancient table acquired from George's mother. The five angels inscribed with our grandchildren's names smiled at us from their new perch on top of the bookcase. The next item I pulled out was precious: the first nativity set my son, Todd, and I bought. We found it at Woolworth's, a five-and-dime store in Minneapolis. Our funds were limited in those days, so the figures were small, and we could afford only one wise man rather than the traditional three. Surprisingly, the sixty-year-old set has survived, except Joseph has a chip on his forehead, which was better than a chip on his shoulder, I suppose.

As I unwrapped each item, George's surprise indicated that he thought it was new. I felt a deep sadness at his loss of memory and connection to the past. He, however, enjoyed the present—which must have been a fun day for him, I imagined—with all the *new* Christmas baubles.

One of my favorite nativity sets is the one with Joseph leading a donkey carrying Mary and baby Jesus. If you look closely, you'll see Jesus is sucking his thumb. It portrays the holy family fleeing the violence of Israel after the birth of Jesus. As any refugee knows, in the midst of fear a thumb can be of comfort to a child. These figures, in all their charm, now sat on our entrance table. Another favorite was on the kitchen counter: my friend Sharon made the stuffed cloth figures, each eight to ten inches tall. I love the funky cow looking adoringly at Jesus in his straw manger.

We once had over fifty nativity sets, many of them gifts. Most are now living in our daughters' homes. A young visitor said, with great appreciation, to one of our daughters, "You sure have a lot of Jesus's family in your house!"

I stood back and looked at the results of my labor. I was glad I decorated and didn't miss this opportunity to walk down memory lane. With memories came enthusiasm for my task. Best of all, George was pleased. Yes, deck the halls. Fa, la, la.

Later, after George was settled in bed, I returned to my chair in the living room, drawn back by the aroma of the gingerbread candle wafting throughout the apartment. I recalled that the Christmas carol has another line: "'Tis the season to be jolly, Fa, la, la, la, la, la, la, la, la."

Decking the halls was one thing, but were we really up to being jolly? In hearing the news of the day, whether it be local, national, or international, one was tempted to forget the holly and jolly of the season. Furthermore, I reflected on our current lives. We were elderly, and George was less physically and mentally able. We had sad days as we missed friends and relatives who had left this earth—and worse, they left us. We were unable to contribute as we once did. Also, we were on the periphery, no longer in the center of action. It wasn't easy to be jolly when we yearned for what was.

With such lingering thoughts, I knew that aging requires one to adapt. Just as I learned that I didn't need a big house to enjoy decorating, I didn't need what once was to enjoy life. Perhaps I could even be jolly. After all, though we were elderly, many people included us in their lives. Our younger friends and relatives lead full, productive lives, yet they took time to show us love. Making new relationships also holds a unique beauty and vitality. While we missed those who were no longer with us, we could focus on relationships with those who were here.

Our contributions, too, were different now. We could encourage the younger generation. We could display a generosity of spirit—and of material goods. We could assist other elderly and, at the other end of the spectrum, pay attention to the little ones. We were no longer the center of activity, but it wasn't many years ago that I craved more time to relax, sit back, and observe. We could do that now as we were not expected to work as we once did. What's not jolly about that?

I looked around our home, taking in its beauty, and focused on the glowing white and silver candle on our table. As its flame dispelled darkness, I felt serene and was reminded of the spirit of hope in the midst of imperfection in ourselves and in the world.

Wherein lies that spirit of hope?

Hope lies in believing God is with us, even in our crises.

Hope lies in expressing goodwill to all people.

Hope lies in working for peace on earth.

When hope resides within us, we can hang the holly and, dare I say, be jolly!

Together, may we hang the moist, shiny, aromatic, living boughs of holly and bring hope and joy to the dark and cobwebbed hallways of the world.

# *18.* THE PROPHET

OUR CHURCH INVITES RETIRED clergy members to read the scripture lesson the Sundays before Christmas. On his Sunday, George inched his way to the pulpit. His journey was long, and the congregation held its collective breath, but he made it. All eyes focused on him as he began, "Reading from the Prophet Isaiah . . ." This old man, reading from a script enlarged for his dim eyes, was once an intense, fiery-eyed prophet himself. His voice, once a cannon in the pulpit, now shook slightly. After he concluded the reading, his weakened body and voice stepped aside.

A young family entered the pulpit. The bright-eyed toddler boy, held in his mother's arms, added his thin, high voice to his mother's as she spoke into the microphone. His big sister hopped around her parents' legs in a disheveled angel costume. Were they two prophets in the making? Their energy was a sharp contrast to that of the aging prophet—the old and the young, the bookends of life.

With assistance, the old man returned to his seat. I looked at him through eyes blurred by rivers of tears and whispered in his ear, "Good job, honey." It reminded me of my comments to our children after a performance. As we left the church, many people approached him and repeated my words, "Good job." Others said, "It was good to see you in the pulpit again." Yes, it was. He had prepared for this responsibility by rehearsing numerous times at home and in the car on the way to church that morning. In rehearsal, his speech was garbled by Alzheimer's at times—but not in the pulpit.

In our usual end-of-the-day routine, I asked him, "How was your day today?"

The tired but pleased old prophet responded, "I was in the pulpit today. It was a good day."

For me, the prophet's wife, it was a day when the sorrow of Alzheimer's was touched by joy.

A few weeks later, the old prophet said, "I feel so sad," as he limped across our living room and carefully deposited himself into his favorite chair. "I feel so sad," he repeated. "This is a sad day today. These books are my dear friends. My history. My journey. They're a part of me." Today was the last big purge of the prophet's tools: his cherished library. He always gave away books every time we moved, but this time he was clearing out almost all of them and saving only a couple of dozen for himself.

We loaded the "dear friends" into a laundry cart and suitcase, both with wheels, because the prophet had an idea for potential new homes for them. The physical and emotional fatigue took a toll, and the prophet now needed a nap. As he sat on the edge of the bed, he looked at me, his eyes weary, and said once again, "I had to say goodbye to some very dear friends today."

We carried out the prophet's idea for new homes for the books the next day. George had invited fourteen younger clergy and lay leaders to gather for a discussion in our apartment building's community room. They came from San Diego to the south, Thousand Oaks to the north, Redlands to the east, and everywhere in between. We sat in a circle as George began our conversation by asking what books we were reading. Next, he segued into his main topic: breaking the silence as an urgent prophetic task of the church.

Several themes emerged in the course of our discussion. We decided that being prophetic was not a mere choice for the clergy but a calling. The attendees identified people they perceived as prophets today. They discussed how the establishment tried to silence contemporary prophets. They asked if the church was complicit with the government. They identified topics of justice that we must support and courageously speak out about. They affirmed how important retired clergy were in the community of silence breakers.

We all enjoyed the wonderful camaraderie, respectful atmosphere, mutual encouragement, and stimulating conversation that left the attendees with new ideas and the courage to become the prophets they felt called to be. Our time together concluded with lunch, but it was obvious that no one was eager to leave.

As for George's books, they were spread out over tables, the piano, and a credenza so the attendees could peruse them and choose any they wanted. I think they loved that George underlined key phrases and made notes in these books; they viewed a used book as a keepsake from him. George had an easier time saying goodbye knowing that his beloved tools of the trade were going to good homes.

The next day, George wrote an email to the attendees:

What can I say? Words seem inadequate to express how happy and blessed I feel after yesterday. Each of you participated so well. Time went by so fast. I still lay in bed thinking of all the good comments and questions that were so provocative. . . . It would be great if more progressive thinkers could feel the energy felt in that room yesterday.

We received numerous emails of gratitude for hosting the gathering.

As for me, I was left with an overflowing heart from all the people who expressed appreciation for George's prophetic ministry. I learned once again that old age could be difficult but also beautiful.

# *19.* THINKING

"GEORGE, YOU NEED TO take your walker so you can use it at the restaurant," I reminded my husband.

"No, I'm not taking it. I don't need it," he said with a touch of impatience.

"George," I said more strongly. "The doctor and our daughters insist that you use it at all times. I'll put it in the car."

"No, Vivian. I'm not taking it," he said, his eyes narrowing. Then, pointing at me with a shake of his finger, in a loud voice, he said, "Vivian, you need to change your thinking!"

One of us needed to change our thinking. I decided to drop the conversation. When he went into the bedroom, I quietly took the walker and put it in the trunk of the car, all the while muttering to myself, "Stubborn Norwegian." When we arrived at our destination, I took it out. He looked at me with puzzlement, as though I were a magician. He used it.

Why did he make a fuss? Here was a man who spent most of his life being in control of schedules, programs, and employees. He made decision after decision on a daily basis in his professional life. Now his decisions were reduced to whether he should use a walker or cane, sleep to ten or eleven in the morning, eat soup or salad, or wear slippers, sandals, or dress shoes. His daily decisions were now pretty mundane, not filled with the excitement of life-changing significance.

The loss of decision making was added to his numerous other losses. He was a man who relished brain stimulation of all kinds. Television writer and Alzheimer's patient David Milch called these losses "an accumulation of indignities."

A few days after the walker episode, George and I discussed a schedule for some upcoming events we were hosting. He wanted to have them right away. I asked, "Why are you pressing me to have them so soon?" I thought the question was reasonable.

With eyes blazing, face contorted, he growled, "Because I'm going to die!"

I was stunned; weakness crept through my body. For him, his outburst was logical; he felt an urgency, a necessity to do things now or it would be too late. His calculations were different than mine. When life is closing down, when the end feels near, urgency is reasonable. As his wife and caregiver, I failed to understand that.

I felt a different urgency. Please, God, give me wisdom for living through these days.

A few days later, I decided to broach the subject. "Sweetheart, the other day you said, 'Because I'm going to die.' Do you think that your death is imminent?"

"I don't know, but I think about it a lot."

"You were angry."

"I know."

"Are you afraid?" I ventured.

"No, but I *am* going to die!"

"I've been with several people at the time of their deaths, including my mom and dad." I wondered if he had forgotten that. "All their deaths were gentle, a gradual leaving. It wasn't frightening. Most deaths are like that. We hear of those that are traumatic, the violent kind. A lingering illness is difficult, but the death is often like being tenderly carried to bed in a parent's arms."

George didn't comment. He looked at me with empty eyes. I wished he would share his feelings more often, but he seemed less capable of doing so than earlier in his disease.

# 20. A LONG LIST OF LOSSES

LOSS IS A PART of life. I watched helplessly as George experienced one loss after another. The following is an organized list that helped me realize the extent of his losses.

## His Prostate

In 2007 George was diagnosed with prostate cancer. He underwent radiation therapy and was able to resume life.

## Kidney Disease

Moderate kidney disease appeared in approximately 2010. It didn't change his lifestyle at the time, but in the decade since, the diagnosis has changed to severe kidney disease in stage five, the final stage. Healthy kidneys were a major loss.

## His Eyes

"Honey, I can't see the ball on the golf course. I can hit it, but I can't see where it lands." George had just walked in after playing golf. He sat in his favorite chair, eyes down, with a look of defeat on his face. "I think I have to give up golf."

I thought it was because golf balls are small. It wasn't surprising that they were hard to see, especially at eighty years of age. My optimism diminished when I learned that he could no longer see a tennis ball. Macular degeneration caused him to reluctantly give up both sports.

Next went driving. The reading of road signs became problematic, but he stubbornly insisted that he was just fine. One evening he drove to a meeting in an area new to him. He returned home later than I'd anticipated. One foot in the door and he shook his head. "Don't *ever* let me do that again!" He explained that he couldn't read the signs in the dark and took several wrong turns that left him unable to decipher where he was. He was lost and felt anxious and panicked. He was surprised that he made it home. Soon he stopped driving, day or night.

George's favorite activity was reading, despite a rocky start. His third-grade teacher claimed that he didn't know how to read after spending first and second grades in a small country school. When his family moved into town and he attended a different school, he quickly made up for lost time. Since adulthood he's been an avid reader, especially theological books. Now with failing sight, he deeply lamented the difficulty he had when reading. He did use a lighted magnifier, and a reading device in the library, as well as had people read to him, but said it wasn't the same. He often said, "You're so lucky to be able to read." Sight is precious. It was a huge loss.

## His Ears

When George finally agreed to a hearing aid, it eased the loss of this important sense. However, his hearing had diminished to the extent that without his hearing aids he could not hear me unless I shouted into his ear. Even with them in he had limited hearing. He used to initiate conversation through questions, and while he still did, due to his loss of hearing he missed what others were saying and drifted off into his own world. Movies weren't much fun because he missed many words. "They talk too fast" he complained. Television held limited enjoyment because he missed much of it, even though he used a special hearing device. The combined loss of hearing and sight compounded the problem.

## His Mobility

It completely surprised me when he began to walk with a shuffle, seemingly unable to pick up his feet, since he was once an athlete. I said, "Honey, you're dragging your feet." My observation wasn't appreciated. "Let me walk the way I want" was his reply. When he began to use his cane, the transition didn't please him. "I don't need it" was his usual retort when its use was suggested. After our daughters and sons-in-law strongly urged him to use a cane, he finally gave in. The same reticence was displayed with the necessity of using a walker and, eventually, a wheelchair. Each transition came with refusal, then acquiescence. It was not easy to feel so dependent.

### His Ability to Use Technology

George's ability to use technology gradually decreased. He was accustomed to using the computer; many hours were spent writing letters and sending and receiving emails. That went by the wayside when he could no longer remember how to use it. He struggled with the phone as well. I became his secretary.

### His Loss of Privacy

Perhaps one of the most sensitive losses involved toileting. Such a private activity can make one feel ashamed when there were problems. First came the need to use special underwear. Then, a big change was the need to self-catheterize. Finally, it was necessary to insert a permanent catheter that was emptied morning and evening either by me or a nurse. When bowel movements and urination became major topics of our conversations, the highlight of my day was if I had the opportunity to visit with a person or two and talk about diverse, pleasant topics. Hospice determined that a nurse needed to assist George with his shower; he objected, arguing against it for twenty minutes. Hospice persisted, and finally he grew to appreciate this act of kindness, readily accepting a shower, a shave, and nail care. Eventually even that changed: a bed bath became the norm.

### His Loss of Memory

"You are so fortunate to have a good memory," George often told me. His memory loss was gradual. First came a diagnosis of mild cognitive impairment, then later, an Alzheimer's diagnosis in 2018. It saddened me when I compared his current memory to the past when he knew all the names of the parishioners in our churches, even those with very large memberships. He also memorized his sermons, often speaking without notes. Now he searched to recall events, people, and places. He reviewed and rehearsed the names of the churches he had pastored, the countries we had visited, the events he had initiated, and people he knew. When he couldn't bring up information he wanted so desperately to remember, I grew sad.

## His Loss of Inhibitions

George's loss of inhibitions probably bothered me and our family more than it bothered him. He seemed oblivious to some of his actions and comments that we found embarrassing and upsetting. He lost filters that guarded against impropriety. At times, others pointed out the inappropriateness of his comments and actions. It appeared that he dismissed such concerns as nonsense.

## His Appetite

George's appetite tanked. "I'm not hungry," he responded every time food was presented. Fortunately, he ate but only half of his former portions. It seemed that his taste and smell diminished, which contributed to his disinterest in food. He continued to lose weight. "Are you hungry?" I asked. "No, I'm never hungry. But I'll try to eat something."

## *His Loss of the Familiar*

One of the changes George fought the most was the switch from a queen-sized bed to twin beds. I needed the change because he developed frequent movements with his hips, legs, and arms throughout the night. I couldn't sleep, and I needed my rest in order to care for him. I researched mattresses and one day took him to a mattress store. I asked him to lie on the mattress that I thought suited him, then asked his opinion. "It's comfortable but we don't need it." He sat on a chair by the door, disinterested, while I dealt with the clerk. I returned to him and said, "They can deliver the twin beds next Monday. Should we go ahead?"

"No. Don't have them delivered until September." That was six months away. I made an executive decision and ordered the beds with delivery for Monday. They arrived on schedule, the old bed was taken away, and George, apparently resigned, decided to try his new bed. The phone rang; the caller was a friend from the past. I put the speakerphone on and told George who was calling. Without a hello or a how are you, George said, "We got twin beds." Our friend didn't respond. George repeated in a louder voice, "We got twin beds." There was another long pause. Not knowing what to say, the caller finally said, "Oh. Uh-huh." The beds were the uppermost thought in George's mind. Surely his friend would think it important too. Later, George's bed was replaced with a hospital bed.

## His Work and Calling

George's profession as a pastor was of utmost importance to him. He was accustomed to being a leader, a decision maker, a speaker—he spoke with power and authority. He was an implementer and writer, a contributor to society. His schedule was the important one and our family lived by it. I wonder if the loss of his profession was his biggest loss.

## Generalized Loss

We can feel loss over a local, national, or international event or condition. Hearing about a tornado in the Midwest, reading about children living in poverty in our own city or a country far away, learning about a life-taking virus like Ebola—such knowledge can lead to a feeling of loss—of security, or of faith in one's government or God.

George was not alone in feeling loss. We all feel some sort of loss, especially as we age. One loss can be unsettling, but numerous losses such as George experienced are like an earthquake. One's entire world is jolted, cracked, and shaken.

While we can always find blessings, let's face it—loss is not easy.

# 21. Troubles from the Outside World

WE HAD A NEW problem: the world was in the middle of a pandemic.

Our city, country, and world were invaded by an infectious disease called COVID-19. In the United States, we first heard about the new disease in January 2020. Six months later it was still spreading. Daily cases rose. Deaths were mounting. Regents Point was taking all the precautions urged by the health authorities. We all practiced hand washing, physical distancing, and mask wearing. All activities and outings were canceled. No visitors were allowed—not even our children—except in emergency situations. Yet the president and his administration floundered in giving our country clear guidelines, even denying science and the seriousness of the virus. Some went so far as to call it a hoax.

I felt the weight of this crisis. I missed the help of my daughters, Joy and Sonja, and my friends who made my work as caregiver more manageable. Fortunately, the hospice caregivers continued to visit twice a week, giving George a bed bath, helping him with pain management, and checking his vital signs. Regents Point nurses also checked George daily. The pandemic made it almost impossible for me to have a respite. Since neither family nor friends could stay with George, I would have to hire a caregiver. However, where would I go? Hotels, theaters, and restaurants weren't safe.

Then, in the midst of this difficult situation, Joy was in a serious accident. The morning had started misty and overcast, but by eleven o'clock, golden fingers of sunshine poked through the clouds and tapped George on the shoulder as he sat in his patio chair. I was excited because Joy and I planned a rendezvous at a nearby grocery store's parking lot. The hospice social worker came to be with George. Joy and I wore our obligatory masks and maintained social distancing. After a great visit, I returned home and planned to join George on the patio. First, I completed a few household chores. I did the usual picking up and putting away and, my most unfavorite, swept the ubiquitous crumbs off the dark wood floor. But, happy day, the golden patio awaited.

When my cell phone rang, I was bummed—I didn't want an intruder to delay my patio rest. However, Joy's husband was identified as the caller, and Stevens was no intruder.

"Joy was in an accident. On the 405 [freeway]," he said with a catch in his throat. "She's alive."

Chunks of fear lumped in my heart. I had just seen Joy. The accident occurred on her way home after leaving me. She was our youngest child, the mother of three and a teacher. Joy personifies her name.

I heard Stevens say, "She's in the UCI trauma center. They won't let Mackenzie [our granddaughter] and me see her due to COVID-19. I'll keep you posted."

My fear grew. This was bad news on top of George's precarious health and the COVID-19 pandemic. I can't deal with one more thing, I thought.

A hospice caregiver came by to see George, trying to determine his source of nighttime pain. I hadn't given the news to George yet. I wanted more information first.

The phone rang again. It was Stevens: "We've learned that Joy has a fracture in her sternum and one at the base of her neck. She has large bruises and abrasions. She *can* talk. She *can* move her arms and legs."

Despite the severity of Joy's injuries, Stevens's report sounded hopeful. When I gave the news to George, the male hospice caregiver took me aside and said, "I know of a guy with injuries like that. He died, suddenly. A couple days after the accident."

Fortunately, George didn't hear him, and I dismissed the comment as the guy was young and, like me, sometimes didn't think before he spoke. Of our children, Joy lived the closest, so she was a major support to us. Now what?

I didn't want to deal with this new development, but I had to. George didn't seem to grasp the serious nature of the accident. He showed sadness but wasn't realistic. Though Joy's car was totaled and she was in the hospital, he kept asking if she was driving again.

Later we learned a lot more. An erratic driver hit Joy's car. Joy's Honda bounced and turned over onto the driver's side, bounced some more, and finally uprighted itself. Four witnesses came to Joy's aid. A man helped open the car door and got her to the side of the road. Three women calmed her, and one called Stevens. Another said, "Look into my eyes. Take deep breaths." The woman who caused the accident wasn't hurt and denied she was at fault. Joy was taken to the hospital, but the witnesses remained to talk to the police and testify to Joy's innocence. We were so grateful for the seat belt and air bags that probably saved her life. Also, credit goes to the four witnesses for stopping, helping, and staying to talk to the police. As Mister Rogers of *Mister Rogers' Neighborhood* said, in a crisis, "look for the helpers."

One week later, neither wild horses nor COVID-19 could keep me from seeing my injured daughter. Though we were discouraged from leaving our villa, I obtained the services of the hospice social worker to sit with George while I hightailed it to Joy's home. I was apprehensive driving the same route Joy had taken on the 405 freeway but managed to hold myself together long enough to safely arrive at Stevens and Joy's home. When I walked in, I wanted to sob and grab my daughter. However, there could be no touching during COVID. I stifled my sobs for

Joy's sake, but if I could have cried internally, my organs would have been drenched. What a relief it was to see her with my own eyes. She would be okay.

It will never again be easy for Joy to feel at ease on the freeway. Tears came when Stevens drove her on the freeway to her first doctor's appointment. She is a calm, emotionally strong person, so I believe that with time she will manage freeway driving once again.

The day of Joy's accident, I didn't have my time of relaxation in the golden sunshine on our patio, but what could be more golden than having one's daughter alive and recovering well.

I would guess that every couple has issues in their lives together. I never met partners who claimed a problem-free union. If they did claim as much, I would question their honesty or whether one of them always gave in to the other. My children were no exception. Sonja and her husband, who was also named Steve, recently had some tumult that centered around something they both enjoyed. They were a couple who found pleasure in exploring the delights of wine. This paired well with Sonja's marvelous cooking skills and the fun they experienced in hosting parties. They were not alone in appreciating wine—Steve's family and ours did as well.

Steve learned that drinking was a problem for him. That, of course, meant that it was a problem for their marriage. I am not a therapist or rehabilitation counselor, but my observations told me that though there may have been multiple reasons for Steve's addiction, the difficulties Steve and Sonja experienced in dealing with their son's problems played a part. Their adopted son, Todd, named after our son who died, struggled with addictions and subsequent aberrant behavior. He moved to Colorado in his twenties and seldom contacted his parents. Helping Todd was extremely difficult. His sixteen-year-old birth mother was unaware of which boyfriend was Todd's birth father, and we suspected one or both of his birth parents used drugs. Steve and Sonja were heartbreakingly disappointed that they couldn't help their son. They tried everything. I could be wrong, but I think Steve's frustration and disappointment contributed to his excessive drinking. Perhaps when he drank, he felt beautifully blurred to any problems.

Steve went to rehabilitation numerous times. Each time, he believed he would be fine, but he continued to drink. Sonja felt great distress and, finally, gave him an ultimatum: "I can no longer trust you. You must leave the house. Do not come back to live with me until you are sober for six months." Steve moved in with his mom. Though he went to rehab several times, he could not last six months without drinking. Nevertheless, he decided to move back in with Sonja. Believing she could not deal with that, she found an apartment and moved there in the beginning of 2020. Steve remained in their home.

The isolation that COVID-19 caused was difficult for all of us but especially so for addicts. Steve drank so heavily that he had to be hospitalized on a couple of occasions because he was ill and dehydrated. Steve finally agreed to rehab once again when a therapist friend arranged for him to enter the acclaimed Betty Ford Center for addiction treatment in Rancho Mirage, California. Steve's brother, Glen, drove him there, got him admitted, and helped him settle in.

Steve returned home after treatment. Sonja saw him on occasion but remained cautious about reuniting. Their future was undecided. George and I remained supportive of both of them. We wanted the best for Steve, a dear person whom we love. We wanted our daughter Sonja to be happy, whole, content, and in a relationship with Steve only if that is the best for her. We love her beyond words.

Here I was at eighty-five wishing I could prevent or heal all life's difficulties and crises for my daughters. Though they were middle-aged women, I wanted to protect them. In reality, in addition to dealing with their own lives, they took on the responsibility of protecting their parents.

# 22. DAILY LIFE

I ADMIT IT—ONE day I became weary of caregiving.

Most days I could swing with it, be upbeat and positive. That day I was weary of the routine and tired of the constant responsibility. I agree with the old saying that the problem with daily life is that it's so daily. It can be mundane. Add caregiving into daily living and you have the constancy of doctors' appointments, procedures, supply orders, and new medications and then putting the needs of the care receiver at the top of your priority list. Yes, daily life is so cotton-pickin' daily!

I didn't need to be reminded of the song that goes "Count your blessings, name them one by one. Count your blessings, see what God has done." I knew I was the recipient of many blessings. When I thought of the big picture—famine, floods, war, refugees—my problems were miniscule. Yet today I just needed five minutes to gripe. In the past, daily life was more interesting because George and I always had something to look forward to. We had the habit of making plans and setting goals, so even when life was difficult, we anticipated a trip, party, conference, or family gathering. Now, with COVID's ugly intrusion into our lives, we had to forgo those social events.

On the positive side of daily living, while recovering from illness or surgery, I yearned for the daily routine permitted by my healthy self. I rejoiced when once again I could make the bed, prepare coffee, and water the plants. Magically, the mundane seemed glorious. I also deeply appreciated the constancy of daily life when the unexpected happened. When life got crazy, I said, "I can't wait to get back to normal." Then the same old, same old brought a sense of security in the midst of troubling change. When everything else seemed turned on its head, the normalcy of making a grilled cheese sandwich was amazingly comforting. Routine has its place in stabilizing one's world.

So, what could I do when I became weary of my routine? Writing helped. Plus, a secret taste of the black cherry ice cream hidden behind the bread in the freezer sounded good. Shhh.

# 23. WHAT DID YOU SAY?

SOMEONE ONCE SAID THAT marriage is two people who spend lots of time calling to each other from different rooms. That person must have had good hearing, as George and I could be in the same room and we still wouldn't hear each other. We spent an inordinate amount of time repeating ourselves. No wonder time seemed to go so fast; we double-talked the days away.

I was happy when my beloved acquired hearing aids. After that, he heard me, but it was obvious that I must not know how to speak clearly. I said, "Honey, it looks like rain today," to which he replied, "What are you saying about wine?" Or I said, "We need to leave in ten minutes," and he asked, "Who?"

It reminded me of the time I said to his mother, "Your hair looks nice." Grandma Gladys squished up her face and said, "My hearing is fine." I tried again: "Grandma, I like your hair. Did you go to the beauty shop?" With a frown and in a louder voice, she set me straight: "I. Said. My. Hearing. Is. Just. Fine!" with each word emphasized like a series of sharp knocks on a door.

Diminished hearing was convenient when the phone rang at night; George didn't have to answer it because without his hearing aids he couldn't hear it. Likewise, the paramedics could have been in our bedroom giving me CPR and George would have slept through it. In our former home, a frightened neighbor knocked on our door at one o'clock in the morning, believing that she was being stalked. I pulled her inside our home and called security while trying to calm her hysterical crying. Two officers came, banging on the door, inadvertently rattling the gear on their equipment belts as they stepped inside, and loudly questioning both of us. My protector slept with the deep sleep of one who had climbed Mount Kilimanjaro that day.

As in other marital situations, flexibility and adaptation were helpful. George was pleased that he could remove his hearing aids and be blissfully undisturbed while I listened to music or a television program. George used a television device called TV Ears that the makers accurately claim saves marriages. With this magical equipment George could listen to television at the volume he preferred, and I at my volume of comfort, or he could turn off the sound so that I could turn my attention to a book or other activity while he still listened.

I'm sad for all those who are hard of hearing, in that it is a serious condition. Table conversations can be difficult; if more than one conversation takes place, it becomes garbled noise and tempts the hard of hearing to give up and withdraw. I cringe when people are impatient with someone dealing with hearing loss as though the person is doing it on purpose to annoy others. I'm told that it becomes embarrassing to ask people to repeat their words, especially if those who are hard of hearing have to ask more than once. They tire of asking people to speak up, and sometimes the problem isn't volume but muddled words and a lack of clarity.

My concern is that those with hearing loss may feel isolated. They can miss hearing important news. Or they may miss just one word that gives meaning to a sentence, leaving them with incorrect information. Another problem is that the hearing impaired may make a comment that was made earlier yet unheard by them. All the foregoing can be embarrassing and may lead to withdrawal from conversations and, worse, withdrawal from social engagement.

Dr. Michele Wilson, who works with audiology, hearing aids, and speech-language pathology, suggests that when speaking with a hard of hearing person we do the following: Make eye contact. Have your face visible to the listener. Let facial expressions and gestures match the spoken information. Speak slowly with key words longer, louder, and higher in pitch.

Wilson doesn't suggest a jab in the ribs and yelling, "Listen to me!" While trying to keep a sense of humor about hearing limitations, we should also be alert, compassionate, and helpful in our interactions. Let's speak up, speak clearly, and refrain from talking over another's comments. In looking the hard of hearing in the eyes, we may see a gleam of gratitude.

In no way do I think diminished hearing is something to make fun of, yet it helped George and me to see humor in the midst of our problems. George once came close to a hearing aid disaster. We were eating a dinner of cashew chicken, one of our favorite indulgences. As we discussed the events of the day, George dropped a cashew on the floor. He reached down and picked it up, decided it was clean enough to eat, and popped it in his mouth. It came flying out like a spitball in math class.

It's best not to chew on your hearing aid!

In his defense, it does resemble a cashew.

# 24. CONVERSATIONS

I PUT MY CELL phone on speaker mode. My husband and his Minnesota sister were about to have a phone visit. I set the volume as high as it could go so George could hear his sister. They're only one year apart in age; consequently, they had many shared experiences. She lived in a lovely facility similar to ours.

George started the conversation, "How are you doing, Gloria?"

"I'm not doing anything. Just sitting here with no company. Nothing."

"Oh." George tried again. "But how are you feeling?"

"What did you say? Did you ask about the weather? It's cold."

"It's nice here. I sit on the patio."

"Well, you're lucky. I have to live here. It's cold, cold, cold."

George's mind moved to the past: "Gloria, who were your girlfriends in high school?"

"Your girlfriend was Esther." She had a bit of indignation in her voice. "Don't you remember?"

"Yes, but who were *your* girlfriends?"

"I told you: Esther. You should remember your girl-friend." Her tone was that of a shaming older sister.

"What? Speak up, Gloria."

The conversation was going nowhere. I decided to insert a different question. "Are your children allowed to visit you, Gloria?"

"Nooo." She drew the word out in slow motion. "This virus has got me stuck in this little room. Can't see nobody. Nobody!"

George asked, "Does the staff bring you your meals?"

"What did you say? I can't hear you, George."

"Do they bring you food?"

"No. Well, they bring me food. It's awful. I can't eat it. They don't cook good like they do at your place. I eat ice cream instead."

And so it went. I thought the conversation was pretty unsatisfactory.

George said later, "It was nice to talk to my sister."

Occasionally, George and I had conversations of length and meaning. However, at this stage of George's illness, our mealtime conversations barely existed. With his head down, he focused on his food, pushed any vegetables to the side, and nibbled on the meat.

I tried drawing him out with what I perceived as topics of interest. "I see you're reading Brueggemann's new book. How is it?"

"He's great." He paused.

"What do you like about him?"

"I guess I like him because he agrees with me." He paused again, then said, "I had a bowel movement today."

"Oh. That's nice." What else could I say?

"I hope I have one tomorrow."

"Uh-huh." I took two sips of wine, then drained the glass.

I passed on dessert: chocolate pudding. George ate his and mine.

Did the content of a conversation, or lack thereof, matter at this time in George's life? I put that question to a few friends. They each responded similarly to our friend and prolific author Walter Brueggemann, whom we greatly admired. Brueggemann wrote, "I think the most important thing to George is that you are with him. That is your greatest gift."

I hoped so.

# 25. An Adventure

A DISTRESSING ASPECT OF George's illness was that he had pain that usually occurred during the night and interrupted his—and my—sleep. Hospice tried pain meds, but he had side effects. With the consent of hospice, I decided to turn to something else. I went on an adventure.

One morning, I searched for a specific number above a building door. There it was. No, that couldn't be it. Was that right? The building looked too nice. I was expecting a small hovel in a string of rundown storefronts. A two-story, contemporary building had the correct number. I decided to check it out. The parking lot was almost full. I quickly turned into the last remaining space.

I felt a tinge of nerves as I grabbed my purse, locked the car, and started for the building. A large sign hung by the entrance door: "No minors. No entrance without a mask. Stand 6 feet apart from other customers. No smoking." And the final warning: "NO firearms!" Okay, I passed the test.

I wondered if I was in the right store. Nothing about its appearance added up based on what I expected of a store that provided what I was looking for: marijuana. Because of my background, marijuana brought up negative images: drug addicts, individuals in trouble with the law, and irresponsible, stoned people. Somehow, even though cannabis use is legal in California, I felt like I was doing something illicit. The image in my head called for dark, dank, and dingy surroundings, with young employees dressed in faded and tattered clothes, munching on spiked brownies. Contrarily, this place was large, sunshine bright, and sparkly clean. It resembled an Apple store, for Pete's sake.

I looked around. The employees—and customers—varied in age and looked like, well, you and me. A professionally dressed woman met me at the check-in counter. She smiled, and her eyes met mine as she said, "Welcome. How may I help you?"

"This is my first time here," I said. (Did she notice the wobble in my voice?)

"Oh, yes, I would be happy to help you. What is it that you need?"

"I'm here to obtain some medicinal cannabis for my husband. He's a hospice patient. He's having pain, and the pain medications give him difficult side effects."

"Sure, I'll help you. I'd like to spend some time explaining the products to you." She quickly called over another employee to assist the line of incoming people forming behind me—six feet apart thankfully. It was obvious that the store had no shortage of customers. Then she led me to another area of the store and opened a computer. Still nervous, I cast a glance over my shoulder—everything looked normal.

"Now, tell me more about your husband's situation." As I spoke, her eyes expressed concern. She offered, "When I was twenty, my mom was ill with cancer and I was her primary caregiver. I wish I would've had medicinal cannabis to help her with pain. She was on hospice until she died. It was so tough for her but also for me, her caregiver. I feel for you. Let's take a look at some potential help for your husband."

She spent considerable time going over the various types of cannabis, plus the different forms in which it comes: oils, edibles, lotions, smokes, patches, inhalers, and more. All the information was on the computer, including the prices. After making my choice, she pointed me upstairs to pick up and pay for my purchase.

A courteous young man showed me the bottle, asked if I had any questions, then explained the dosage. When I brought my credit card out, he said, "Cash only, please." I didn't have enough cash due to the high city and state taxes that were added to the initial cost.

"No problem," he said and pointed me to an ATM just across the aisle. (Apparently, cannabis dispensaries can't acquire bank accounts and therefore can't accept credit cards because the federal government, unlike California and other states, doesn't recognize cannabis as legal.) I paid, took my legal purchase in my hot hand, and left.

The parking lot was still full. Interestingly, the dispensary was considered "an essential business" during the pandemic. Before I went on this adventure, I conferred with some trusted family and friends, plus a couple of physicians and nurses. They didn't discourage me and confirmed that many patients on cannabis were relieved of pain and other discomforts.

Now we would put cannabis to the test. I hoped it would be the pain reliever my husband needed. To my relief, the adventure was not shameful. And if cannabis were effective, hallelujah!

The cannabis was partly effective but not sufficiently so. George still had pain. Hospice suggested the use of a pain-relief patch on his abdomen. That was more effective, especially when used in combination with hydrocodone-acetaminophen, another pain medication. I learned that pain management is a trial-and-error proposition. Fortunately, George finally had relief.

# 26. A New Kind of Reality

ANOTHER PROBLEM OCCURRED: GEORGE began to hallucinate. Maybe it was caused by Alzheimer's, kidney disease, or medications or a combination of all three. Whatever the cause, hallucinations became a part of our lives. They were George's reality. In a more lucid moment, he said, "My mind is playing tricks on me these days."

I responded, "That must be confusing. Would you like to talk about it?"

He replied, "I need to rest now. Let's talk about it tomorrow." We didn't.

Around one o'clock one morning, George sat on the edge of his bed and said, "We have to get our things. The Budapest driver is waiting for us." He was agitated and beckoned me with one arm.

I tried to orient him to reality. "Honey, we're in our own little house, not in Budapest."

"Vivian, be sensible! I know the truth. You don't. We're in Budapest." He reached for his walker. "Get ready. We have to go."

Though weak, George pushed past me with his walker and went straight to the front door. I managed to stop him and tried to distract him. He'd have none of it and tried to move past me. "See all those people out there?" He pointed out the window. "They're waiting for us."

I decided to play along. "I'll talk to them." I waved at the imaginary people and yelled, "Thanks for coming. Bye." Then to George, "They left, honey. They had some other place to go." I urged him to return to his cozy bed.

As I tucked him in, he said, "We're not in California. We're in Budapest." He had the last word.

About two hours later, George awoke and pointed at "all those kittens on our floor." Next he said, "There's water all over the floor," and then, "Sweep up all those leaves. They cover the floor." I felt jerked between irritation and sadness, frustration and sympathy.

The hallucinations continued for twenty-four hours. He slept for a few minutes, awoke suddenly with a jerk, then stared at the ceiling or floor. At one point he managed to get up, wobbled over to the dresser, and removed two pairs of pajamas. "We've got to pack. They're coming to get us, Vivian. Hurry up."

He and I were exhausted after a sleepless night and tumultuous day. I called for a caregiver for the next two nights, allowing me a decent sleep on the couch. George slept twenty-two out of twenty-four hours for each of the next three days. I managed to wake him long enough for a cup of soup and his pills each day. When I tried to get him up, he said, "I need to rest. Let me sleep."

One morning, George looked at me as I stood by his bed and asked, "Is Vivian awake yet?" I put my hand on his chest and said, "Sweetheart, I'm Vivian. I'm awake." He recognized me and said, "I thought you were my sister, Ruth. Is Joe here? How about Jimmy?" These comments were about his siblings and his nephew Jimmy, who grew up on a farm that George often visited. George turned his thoughts to the farm and said with urgency, "We have to fertilize the corn." I suggested that we do that tomorrow.

Frequently the hallucinations were about his work. "I have a theological paper to write. Four people are helping me. They're spending the night. Where are they sleeping?" Or, "I need a pencil. I have to change the order of service for church today." Or another, "I have a wedding. I can't find the bride and groom."

George had one hallucination that was both touching and reminiscent of the past when he was the director of the world hunger program for our national church organization. His words indicated that he believed his staff was with him. George sat up in bed, stretched out his long arm in a semicircle, and said, "It's so nice to have all of you here." His voice was low and slurred yet very tender.

"I want you to know I have confidence in you. Each of you has unique abilities. We need to ask ourselves, What are the expectations that the church has of us? Ask yourself that question today before we go to Washington, DC." He paused for a few minutes as though he was giving them time to think, then continued. "I hope you have confidence in me. But I need to be honest with you: I have Alzheimer's. Severe kidney disease. I can't hear or see very well. The day will come when I need to step down. I hope you will give respect to your new leader." Another long pause. "It was so good to have you here today." The meeting was over, and he went back to sleep. George's lucidity while hallucinating was remarkable. The tenderness he expressed was so beautiful that I was tearful all day. This was the kind man I married.

One day George insisted that I send emails for him. I used my laptop and pretended to be typing as he dictated mumble-jumble messages to mumble-jumble names. Another day he asked me to draw lines on a paper to make eleven even spaces. Satisfied, he then wanted another sheet of paper to do some "figuring." He sat up in bed with a felt pen and paper and worked for about an hour. The result was a page full of numbers, mostly eleven and forty-five, randomly placed throughout. He never used the sheet with eleven spaces. Whenever I accommodated his requests, usually only pretending to do so, he was satisfied and moved on to other thoughts.

I found one of George's hallucinations funny yet poignant. He had had a catheter for ten months, so he didn't need to use the toilet to urinate. Nevertheless, one evening he beckoned me to his bed and in a conspiratorial whisper said, "Honey, I just went to the toilet. I put my penis on a shelf. Would you go get it for me?"

"Okay," I said. I pursed my lips to keep from laughing and thought, Oh brother, now I've heard it all. If it were true, I suppose I could use super glue. They say it can fix anything. His request was symbolic: with a catheter and lack of energy, sexual activity had ceased. His penis and sex life were on the shelf. He wanted them back.

Another day George called me to his bedside and said, "Vivian, who are all these people by my bed? They've been here all morning. They just stand there. They don't say anything." Then, in a whisper so they wouldn't hear, he said, "I think they have mental problems."

I nodded, thinking somebody in this room did.

## 27. RESTLESSNESS

HAVE YOU EVER FELT deep unrest in the soft folds of your soul?

The unrest I felt was due to George's illness: he was in stage five of kidney disease, the final stage. *Final stage—* what does that really mean?

George, the subject of my unrest, was resting in his favorite chair on the patio. He didn't appear troubled but warm and content in his pajamas and robe, bathed in sunshine. I watched him close his eyes and saw the slight rise of his chest; I watched him nap with nary a care. I was the one in turmoil.

I couldn't sleep the night before due to the unknowns surrounding George's condition. At this final stage of kidney disease, should we go on as usual? Or should we do something different? I mentally checked off a list:

- We didn't need to discuss finances. We'd done that. Unlike some women, I had a grasp of our finances since I'd been the taking-care-of-money person for the past thirty years.

- We didn't need to discuss burials. We'd made arrangements to donate our bodies to the UCI medical school; the school would be notified at the time of our deaths and would take care of all the details.

- We'd discussed a memorial service, not with great detail, but all the important decisions were in writing. It made me sad that George's service would have to wait until the pandemic was over. How long that would be, nobody knows.

I struggled with the less tangible, such as missing our deeper, poignant conversations. The reality was that Alzheimer's impacted conversation. While George still communicated, something was missing, not only memory but the full personality that I knew for sixty years. That's why I felt an absence of the understanding and depth we once enjoyed in conversing. Our conversations were now dull and dry. The juice was missing.

We tried to do something fun or different each day. I took George out for car rides, looked through photo albums with him, and helped him compose letters, but what was I missing? I kept thinking I should do more, but I didn't know what that more was. Were there ways to interact now to prevent having regrets later?

My questions were normal according to author Pauline Boss. In her book *Loving Someone Who Has Dementia*, she helped me understand that with a dementia diagnosis the patient was both present and absent. Such duality was confusing; to make sense of a nonsensical situation became challenging. Boss explains how life is dramatically altered because the relationship as you knew it is ruptured. The loss is ambiguous, one that is unclear with no resolution or closure. The caregiver also wrestles with not knowing what is coming next or when and how it will end. Could I let go of feeling guilty for not knowing how to handle everything? If I could become comfortable with a less-than-perfect solution and relationship, perhaps that clarity in the midst of ambiguity would give me peace.

With George's kidney diagnosis, his remaining time was unknown. Some people lived a few weeks, others a year. Life gives us many mysteries, death being one of them. How imminent was death? Where was death? Was it waiting outside the bedroom door? Was it lurking in the corner of the bedroom? Or was it close, sitting on the foot of the bed? What would it be like—a roaring lion or a purring kitten? Would it be a struggle or a gentle transition into a different sphere?

It was still possible that I could die first. I was strong, but I could have a heart attack, an accident, or something else. A startling statistic is that caregivers die at a rate 63 percent higher than people the same age who are not caring for someone with dementia. However, if I outlived George, what would life be like without him, without his physical presence? I knew that I would greatly miss George and would need to draw on memories to sustain me. I prayed that the memories we made now would add joy to the future.

I often turn to the written word for solace and new thoughts. That day, I absorbed the words of May Sarton. She wrote of moving toward a new freedom, of learning to let go, and of the sweetness that letting go brings. I was trying to let go of the unknowns, to live in the moment and move to a new freedom. When I did so, it was sweet grace to my restless soul.

# 28. THE BENEDICTION

A WEEK BEFORE THE COVID-19 shutdown, George and I hosted a clergy seminar. Twenty participants came for a day of presentations, dialogues, and brainstorming.

At the end of the day, George raised his thin arms. In a whisper of a voice and while seated in a wheelchair, he prayed the benediction over those of us attending the seminar:

> May the Lord bless you and keep you.
> May the Lord's face shine upon you.
> May the Lord's countenance be lifted upon you,
> and give you peace.

The words, and the heart from which they came, brought moisture to my eyes that then slipped down my cheeks. George had been my husband and a pastor for sixty years. After all those years of ministry and pronouncing the benediction, I wondered if this would be his last.

What is it about the benediction that touches hearts? For me, it is ointment on my wounds caused by the difficulties of life. We live in a world that is random, chaotic, and messy. It is random in that a tornado could destroy four houses on your block, yet yours remained untouched. Random in that one child was born into a poverty-stricken family, another into a wealthy one. Random in that a pandemic inserted its ugly head into our lives, infecting some, killing others.

Life is also chaotic in that you could have carefully planned your financial security, then the stock market crashed or a spouse had a serious illness, and the finances flew out the window. Chaotic in that you might have the job of your dreams, then there was a merger of companies where employees got the shaft. Chaotic in that when we needed national leadership, it was lacking.

Unfortunately, life is not only random and chaotic, it is also messy, often due to personal choices. Messy because you chose an occupation and learned that you hated it. Messy because you bought the house of your dreams and found that your next-door neighbor was less than ideal. Messy because you didn't like your in-laws, roommate, or coworker. How do we make sense of such a world and such a life?

Some people find an answer in religion or faith. Belief in God gives those people meaning and purpose in life, especially if they believe that God values and loves them. The words of the benediction "May the Lord's face shine upon you" suggest that God finds pleasure and favor with people. People of faith believe they are in God's hands, as declared in the popular song "He's Got the Whole World in His Hands." If they believe that God cares about the world—and its people—that doesn't necessarily remove the randomness, chaos, and mess, but it may offer comfort and perspective.

Contrarily, some people believe that we invented religion as a way to cope with life in this world. That may be true; it seems plausible to me. My question is, If a person receives peace, comfort, and positive direction through religious belief, is it not helpful—even if religion is invented?

On my faith journey, as the wife of a pastor and after long years of ministering in the church, I had become uneasy with certitudes. I heard some people claim with certainty, "God wants everyone to believe as I do," or, "Religious people are moral," as though the nonreligious couldn't be. How was it that some people believed they had the whole truth? As I heard a theologian say, "If people claim that they know with certainty all about God and God's will, it shows that they know very little about the nature of God." Holy books such as the Bible are not science books or books with answers that address all our contemporary issues. They are books revealing ancient people's thoughts about God. I'm so grateful that we have been given intellectual and intuitive abilities that can be used to explore the deep areas of life, wrestle with questions and doubt, contemplate, and meditate. What a gift it is to not have to know all the answers.

And if people, after exploration and life experience, deduce that there is no God, who am I to claim otherwise for them? For me, it is helpful to believe that there was a wise teacher named Jesus who taught us to love, forgive, work for justice, help the vulnerable, and live in peace. Was he God? I don't know. But I do appreciate that he taught us how to live in this world. People of other faiths—Jews, Muslims, and Hindus, to name some—also receive guidance from their holy books and people of wisdom. In my experience, nonbelievers may also have a moral compass in their hearts that guides them in the path of loving concern for others.

I was grateful for these beautiful words of the benediction, this prayer of blessing found in the Bible. I needed to hear these words. For me, the words "and give you peace" were so comforting and reassuring that I felt safe, calm, and blessedly at peace in the midst of our random, chaotic, and messy world. If we each lived by these words—blessing, keeping, shining, and giving—we would bring peace, wonderful peace, into our lives and into our wounded world.

And to you, George, my loving husband and good and faithful servant:

May the Lord bless you and keep you.
May the Lord's face shine upon you.
May the Lord's countenance be lifted upon you,
and give you peace.

# 29. A Song in the Night

AT MIDNIGHT WHEN IT was as dark as chocolate, I heard George, in a weak, raspy voice, sing,

> Be near me, Lord Jesus, I ask you to stay
> Close by me forever and love me, I pray.

A long pause, and then,

> Bless all the dear children in your tender care
> And fit us for heaven to live with you there.

My face was wet with tears, just as it is whenever I think about it. Those beautiful words, the last verse of "Away in a Manger," came from George's wrinkled lips as he lay in a hospital bed next to my bed in our cozy apartment. His mind was wrinkled, too, with hallucinations and dementia, yet every word of the song slipped through the wrinkles in his brain and became a midnight gift to my worn body and troubled soul.

In recent evenings, to quell George's agitation, I put my laptop near him and played music, either classical or religious. I sat by the bed and held his hand as the soothing tones took both of us into a calm space, preparing us for nighttime. After hearing him sing, I started to use my own voice on occasion to sing to him. I chose some of our favorite songs, hoping maybe, just maybe, he would join me.

As I listened to him sing, my mind wandered to the past. How many times had George sung this song? He most likely learned it as a child in Sunday school or in his childhood home. He must have sung it every year as a pastor while leading Christmas services. Certainly, he sang it with our own children and me beside our Christmas tree. Though always beautiful, to my ears it was never as exquisite as it was that night.

A hymn by Mary Louise Bringle called "When Memory Fades" speaks of old age as a time of many losses yet also as a time when love remains. The words of the hymn describe George: a faded memory, faulty recognition, dimmed eyes, and a confused mind. Yet his spirit remains strong. Through his song in the deep of the night, George spoke to my soul. He spoke of love—his love and the unaltering and unfaltering love of God.

# *30.* CHANGES

GEORGE HAD BEEN UNDER hospice care for nine months; the past month he appeared relatively stable.

## *Saturday, September 5*

I felt a change. Was it the atmosphere or the milieu? What gave a new feel to the room? Though our bedroom always had a calming effect on me, that day it felt quieter, as if it were closing down yet somehow expectant, like closing the door to one room and entering another. Then I realized that the change had to do with George. Our home was changing because he was changing. So was I. Grief was beginning to wrap her arms around me.

The day was ordinary in many respects. George slept for about twenty-two hours, ate a bowl of Cheerios, and drank water and juice, and a nurse checked his vitals. He awakened for a visit with our friend Bob, who read to him from a book of Buddhist poems. Later he helped George autograph a few of his books. As Bob left, George said in a voice so soft, a whisper, "I liked Bob's visit." Then, having spent his energy, he slept once again.

The day before, George thought it was Christmas Eve. He said we had to hurry, get dressed, and get to the church because he had to give a sermon. Another day he needed a pen and paper to take attendance. Yet another, we needed to hurry to an ordination service. The stillness of his body was deceptive as his mind was anything but still. It flew from one topic to another like a drone delivering verbal packages.

## Sunday, September 6

It was six o'clock in the morning. I sat on the patio with Saturday's leftover coffee in hand. The night sky was gray-blue, its eastern edges pushed light into the darkness. A hush descended as pink light spread across the sky like drops of water spreading across a paper towel—soundless but effective. The foliage surrounding my patio sipped water droplets delivered by the sprinklers, their morning coffee.

I heard the waking-up sounds—the engine of a distant truck, a closing door. Irvine, California, was stretching and yawning, preparing for another day. Aromas of a new morning filled my nostrils: the moist earthy smell emitted from the soil, the salty tang of a neighbor's breakfast bacon, the pungent aroma of my cup of coffee.

Moments on the patio gave me strength for my changing world. Throughout the night, George had been restless in body and spirit. At midnight he asked, "Vivian, where have you been?"

"Sleeping," I responded.

"How could you sleep with all of these little children here?"

I assured him that we were alone and it was the middle of the night. It was time to sleep. He was satisfied until four in the morning. Then he said we needed to get dressed and get over to the church for "a meeting." I said the meeting was canceled.

It wasn't the most restful night. Now it was a new day. I reached for the day like fingers reach for medicine, partly grateful, partly tentative. What would the day bring? Change was in the air.

## Friday, September 11

George had problems that day. He had difficulty writing his signature. He also forgot his date of birth. Both lapses of memory bothered me. Aren't our signatures and birthdates an integral part of who we are? How many times in our life have we used them?

It was another sign of the slipping away of my man. I didn't like it.

## Wednesday, September 16

Why do things have to be so difficult? I tried to transfer money from an investment to our checking account to pay for the caregiving services we have three afternoons a week. The bodiless voice on the phone said I needed a power of attorney (POA) document. That's easy, I thought. I sent seventeen copied pages of our revocable trust, which listed me as POA. That wasn't enough, the lawyers wouldn't accept that. I cried. I didn't have the energy to pursue the POA that day. I never did.

When I checked on George, he wanted paper and pen because "I have to take roll call. I can't find my attendance sheet."

"That's okay," I assured him. "You're not going to have class today."

"Oh." That satisfied him. Later, he said, "I have to go to a Lutheran World Federation meeting."

I told him it was canceled due to COVID-19. "Oh," he said, once again satisfied that I knew the score.

## Friday, September 18

"I have to get a part-time job," George informed me. I assured him that our finances were fine and he could rest and not worry about that. I wondered what went on in George's brain. I wished I knew how to help him deal with hallucinations other than to reassure him that he was safe and all was well.

## Saturday, September 19

Today was my eighty-fifth birthday. I hired a caregiver for six hours so I could spend the day with our daughter Joy. It was wonderful, I felt free. We had brunch at an Italian restaurant with delicious food and a patio setting that provided us great privacy—a prized arrangement due to the importance of social distancing at this time of the coronavirus pandemic. Then, we spent the afternoon wandering around the idyllic Sherman Gardens, viewing common and exotic plants. We concluded with a glass of wine in the gardens' bistro, and Joy also had a banana chocolate crepe.

We made plans to celebrate with my other daughter, Sonja, later in October. We'd celebrate Joy's birthday then as well as mine. We three had absolutely stunning times together. It was something to look forward to.

## Sunday, September 20

George's birthday, his eighty-seventh, was a birthday like no other. At midnight on the day, he became agitated. First, he vomited. Fortunately, the contents were mainly liquid, but I still had a wet mess to clean up. After cleaning him and changing the bed, I returned to bed, but George wasn't ready to settle down. The following twenty-four hours were filled with hallucinations. He threw off all his bedding and tried to get up. I was grateful that the railing on the hospital bed prevented that.

George began to elicit help. Calling out to imaginary people, he said, "We need some volunteers here. I want to get up. Are you willing to help?" Next he gave orders. "Stand there. Put your hands here. Push my back here, like this. Good. Try again. You've almost got it."

I got out of bed and intervened, "Honey, you are not getting out of bed. The doctor said you cannot get up because you fall very easily." His lack of understanding of this restriction, and the fact that he managed to get his left leg over the railing, added to my anxiety. We didn't need to deal with an injury on top of everything else.

"We've got to catch the train." He was insistent. I said there was no train. He looked glum. "No train? I'm sorry to disappoint the helpers. You helpers can go now," he said as he motioned for people to leave.

In the hours nearing sunrise, he said, "I'm going to ask my sister Beatrice to play one verse of 'It Came upon the Midnight Clear.'" Moments later, "Our next song is 'O Holy Night' on page 134. One-three-four. I'm sorry. Page 234. Two-three-four. Bea, could you play that for us?"

The next morning, he said, "I had a sing-along last night. It was a flop. I couldn't get anyone to sing."

His hallucinations went on and on for twenty-four hours. Then he slept and slept.

I woke him that afternoon for a birthday surprise: a man from our church came to sing to George. He sang love songs, show tunes, and classical pieces and ended with a beautiful rendition of "The Lord's Prayer"—all a cappella. After singing in the bedroom, he moved to the patio and sang for our neighbors. It was a rare treat, but George showed almost no emotion, as though he was an empty container. I felt sad for him but more so for me.

## Monday through Friday, September 21 through 25

George was not interested in eating. Tuesday, he ate four teaspoons of ice cream. Wednesday, he swallowed three teaspoons of Cheerios. Then he stopped eating. Water was his only intake. I wondered how long he could go without food. Yet his heart was strong. Maybe he'd start to eat again. His mother lived to be 101 years old. I decided to override my optimism and face reality: I sent an email to our families suggesting that they should visit soon if they wanted to see George.

My thoughts went to our son, Todd, and his last days those many years ago. To have watched his strong teenage body deteriorate was brutal. I remembered him whispering to a visitor, "I'm dying, you know." His death was such a painful experience that it overshadowed any other sadness of my life. Each time that I looked at George and thought about Todd, a guttural sob from deep within rose to the surface.

We learned today that our hospice care coordinator had resigned from the hospice service provider. She had told us that she was going on vacation, so we were surprised when we learned that she had resigned. Apparently, she gave the vacation story to all patients and families as well as to other staff. We would miss her as we had grown fond of her. Her leaving was disappointing.

## Saturday and Sunday, September 26 and 27

George still had no interest in food. Getting him to take pills was difficult. He swallowed three of the eight, then shook his head. Fortunately, he had pain relief through the patch on his abdomen. He had greatly deteriorated. George was a six-foot-tall man who barely fit on the length of the hospital bed. Now his long limbs were spindly thin. We couldn't weigh him, but I think he had lost 60 pounds off his 180-pound body, maybe more. He developed a sore on his right heel from the frequent movement of his legs. Hospice was able to prevent it from worsening and kept him free of bedsores.

I was relieved that Joy was able to visit on Sunday. She and Sonja are such bright spots in my life that things always seem better when they appear. Thankfully, Sonja planned to come on Tuesday. Joy as a teacher and Sonja as an occupational therapist found it difficult to get away from their work. I was so grateful when they could.

George had a vomiting spell, mainly liquids and mucus because of his lack of food intake. His bowels released only mucus as well. Nevertheless, it was a wet mess to clean up. Later in the evening he had a second vomiting spell, but I was able to provide a pan in sufficient time. We had a few more of George's books to autograph that I tried to help him sign, but it was to no avail as he could no longer write. I forged his initials instead.

Hospice came and said he was in transition between life and death and that nurses would visit every day. Nurse Lynn suggested he need not take any pills as long as he had the medicinal patch to cover his pain. We were to follow his lead in regard to food and drink. He no longer wanted food and seldom asked for water. I felt numb.

## *Monday through Friday, September 28 through October 2*

Yes, George was in transition, but my second cousin, Ellen, pointed out that I was too. When he died, this would be the first time in my eighty-five years that I would live alone. It would be the first time in sixty years that I would live without my husband. It would be the first time that my life would not revolve around my husband's schedule, desires, and needs.

My Swedish friend Barbro wrote that when her husband was in the dying process, she found she had, oddly enough, a stronger consciousness of life. I could relate to that. In an attempt to face reality, I started a list titled "My Future." Some of the listed items are mundane, some exciting, and some probably undoable. I can dream, can't I?

Because George was declining, a few visitors were allowed despite the pandemic restrictions. On Monday, we had two sets of visitors, all from George's family: his nephew Mark and brother Joe, both clergy, and Joe's wife, Judy. They each prayed and recited scripture, and Joe anointed George's head with oil. Visitors were restricted to forty-five minutes, which was probably wise as George and I got tired from long visits. While face masks and physical distancing were urged for all visitors, we were allowed to touch because of George's closeness to death. Restrictions were distressing at a time when physical touch meant so much. Yet we were thankful for the caring staff and community that wanted to protect us.

Tuesday, Jean and Patty, friends from our church, came bearing gifts. George was blessedly lucid when they were here. He thanked them for being church members who were concerned about justice. He told them to take care of me when he died. Then he told me to take care of them.

After they left, I took advantage of his lucidity to praise him for his steadfast advocacy for social justice. I reminded him that despite being in a wheelchair, he joined me in June for a vigil held by people from our community. Our group banner read Seniors for Racial Justice, and the banner George held said Silence Is Violence. The peaceful vigil protested the murder of yet another African American man, George Floyd, killed by a police officer. After being reminded of the vigil event, George said, "That was a good thing to do. That was the right thing to do."

Sonja arrived around five in the evening. She and I had wine and crackers with a tasty spread of avocados and jalapeños, another Trader Joe's specialty. That was followed with our Regents Point dinner delivered to our villa. I told Sonja how I felt guilty and sad each evening as I ate dinner in candlelight while George did not have the strength or interest to join me. I added that he didn't appear to miss it, but I missed him.

Sonja was able to have some conversation with her dad. He pointed to her, then looked at me and with a thumbs-up said, "She's okay." When his sly humor appeared, it was like seeing a shadowed piece of his former self. It was moving to see our daughters sit by their father's bed with tender eyes, caressing his arm and speaking loving words to him. Sonja spent the night. I didn't want her to leave in the morning, but she had other responsibilities. She reminded me that if I needed her, she would drop everything and come night or day.

Domini, one of our caregivers, rubbed George with lotion and gave him a backrub one afternoon. She did my laundry, watered the outside pots, swept the floor, and took out the trash. All the caregivers did those chores, so I was very fortunate. I suggested to the others that they also rub lotion on George and give him a backrub. Its calming effect was obvious; he fell asleep.

I was tired that day as George had woken me at eleven at night and two and four in the morning. He threw off all his bedding and claimed he had to get up to take care of many things. Once it was "I need to mail some packages," then "I have to go to the store for ice cream," and finally, "It's hard to get good service here. Can you help me?" I was becoming a genius at distracting him and reassuring him that I'd take care of his current need.

Thursday, the first day of October, was a full day. We had no time for a nap. Our friend Sharon called in the morning. It was important for us to catch up with each other. Though she lived in Minnesota, she was walking this journey with us. When Jared and Shelly came, George was lucid. It was an emotional visit with many tears. They were so grateful for George's influence, claiming that he changed their lives and helped them see beyond the "me and God" concept and embrace the social justice aspect of Jesus's ministry.

Sarah, our pastor of only a few days, also visited. She was graciously concerned that she as a new person in our lives did not impose on this sacred time. It was no imposition as I wanted her here. She was our pastor now, and I wanted her to know and share this life-changing event.

Every Thursday at two in the afternoon, I met on Zoom with my caregivers' support group. Corby, our social worker, and Carole, our chaplain, facilitated it. Group members left as spouses died but were replaced with others so that approximately six to eight of us met each time. We used to meet in person, but since COVID we met by Zoom. I felt grateful and close to the group as we learned from each other and from our facilitators.

When our hospice nurse, Lynn, came that day, it was decided to start small doses of morphine for George as he complained of pain in his penis again. He slept very well after receiving that dosage, including through the night.

Friday, George's ninth day without food, started out with him asking me, "When will the changing of water into wine happen?"

I replied, "Jesus did that. It says so in the Bible."

George said, "We've got to get set up for that."

"Okay," I said. "I'll take care of it."

Today I met our granddaughter Mackenzie for lunch while the caregiver was here. We always have good conversations. She is heavily interested in environmental issues, as am I. During the pandemic, she learned via the internet to make several crafts, including clay earrings and macrame decorations. She gave me a macrame coaster, which I cherished. It was a refreshing distraction to meet with her. Four grandchildren—Marie, Andy, Mackenzie, and Matt—came to visit George, whom they called Bumpa, during his dying days. Unfortunately, grandson Todd was still using drugs and living on the streets in Colorado.

## Saturday and Sunday, October 3 and 4

We had another great visit, this time with Cheryl and Eduardo, who is from Venezuela. Eduardo, a mathematics professor, and Cheryl, a children's speech therapist, were so tender and appreciative in talking with George. Eduardo considered George to be one of his mentors. George gave him a Brueggemann book soon after meeting him that influenced Eduardo to begin seminary. He said he "loves, loves, loves" George's new book, *Silence Is Not the Answer,* and had given many copies to friends and students. They brought us a glistening glass apple. It beautifully graces our coffee table and will remind me of their visit each time I gaze on it. As they left, they asked if I needed anything from the store. They drove off and kindly returned with the items I needed, plus several treats.

George slept well again, as did I. Each day he received morphine at nine in the morning and three in the afternoon. This had calmed him and reduced the hallucinations.

I got up around 4:30 in the morning. I felt rested and it was a good time to read or write. I read a booklet provided by hospice, *Gone from My Sight: The Dying Experience* by Barbara Karnes. She offers some guidelines and signs to watch for before death. I recognized some of them in George; others might come later. Karnes indicated that people are different, of course, so not all have the same signs.

I printed out two hundred pages of a manuscript that I was working on. It was my life story beginning with my birth, tentatively titled *The Willow Tree and Me: A Memoir*. I wanted both daughters to read it to check for inaccuracies, as well as for stories they wished were included and for anything that may be hurtful. My plan was to finish it after George's death.

It was a difficult visit for Joy. To see one's father so ill, so close to death, is hard enough. But then there were issues regarding her teaching job plus the ups and downs of daily life. The pandemic added extra layers of stress. Sonja had her own struggles as she was going through a divorce with Steve, her husband of thirty-five years. Her work in the hospital was impacted by the coronavirus, making her days more tense than usual. She was adjusting to living alone in an apartment as well as trying to plan her future while simultaneously dealing with her daddy's death. It was close to being too much. I thought my mother's heart must keep beating for my darling daughters.

Some say that there is a thin veil between heaven and earth. If so, I was trying to peek back and forth, from one side to the other. A friend wrote, "At a certain point the dying are much closer to God than they are to us." I contemplated those words.

Two couples came for short visits in the afternoon. Jeanne and Frank were new to our community. She played her guitar and she, Frank, and I sang some religious songs from our backgrounds, such as "Softly and Tenderly" and "Jesus Loves Me." They left, and Virginia and Bob arrived. They were dear friends; it was sad for all of us to see George so ill and to realize that he was leaving us. As a friend said, "So many of us continue to walk George home."

It had been a full day. Five visitors and four medical people. I went to sleep at eight o'clock.

## Monday, October 5

It was day twelve of no food for George. I rubbed his hands, arms, neck, and head with a soothing lotion, swabbed his mouth with a citrus-flavored swab, and whispered good morning to him.

The nurses who provided good care for George experienced emotional involvement, especially those who worked more often with him. Observing his decline reminded them of family deaths and of other residents' deaths. Their emotions peeked through their professional manner, similar to a teacher touching a hurting child on the shoulder and allowing a sole tear to escape from his or her eye. Such emotional involvement with us endeared them to me; I did not see it as unprofessional.

## Tuesday, October 6

"I can't breathe" were George's barely perceptible words as I came to him straight from my bed at seven in the morning. I called hospice and our nurses' clinic. Together, they determined he needed more morphine, and a nurse came immediately to administer it. That quieted him and his breathing became regular though shallow. Hospice nurses were helpful in reminding me of what to expect as George approached death. I appreciated this information as I am the type of person who wants to know the facts. Not all people do. Some, in not knowing, find comfort. Perhaps they feel it's not happening if they don't know what to look for.

Our hospice nurse rebandaged the sore on George's heel, checked his vitals, and cleaned his mouth and other areas. She freshened him. That she cared so well for his body was an act of compassion. The focus was on comfort and pain-free care.

What a treat I had that day. Karla, our pastor of several years ago, brought a lunch of delicious Mexican food, my favorite. Before we indulged, she went into the bedroom to visit George. Her angel voice filled the room as she sang "How Great Thou Art," the song we had claimed as "our" song when we were dating. Following lunch, she once again sang to George. While holding his hands and with closed eyes, the words of "Our Father" left her lips and flowed into our very beings, bringing light that eased the stress and pain of our days. Later, the memory of it reminded me of the lyrics of the Stevie Wonder song "Never in Your Sun" sent to me by a friend. Wonder wrote of relieving someone's pain in pouring rain, never in the sun. Karla brought me relief during the pouring rain of pain.

The day concluded with a phone call from dear friends Su and Hank. I held the phone to George's ear as they spoke beautiful, loving words to him. He was unable to respond, but he heard their gratitude for him. They have the hope of establishing a fund in memory of George to assist students in experiential travel to Israel and Palestine or other destinations. I put them in touch with Thom, our Claremont School of Theology professor friend. I'm pretty excited as these folks—Su, Hank, and Thom—are can-do people!

## Wednesday, October 7

It had been two weeks since George had eaten. His body was so diminished that when I looked at him my eyes hurt. He was a person of good health and physique for most of his life. I felt such sadness in seeing his emaciated and spent body. I prayed that he didn't ask me for a mirror. How much longer, Lord?

Steve, our son-in-law, came through the door carrying his guitar and a smile. There was a poignancy in his visit as he and our daughter Sonja were in the process of a divorce. Nevertheless, we loved him and considered him part of our family. He played several songs by George's bedside, ending with "The Little Drummer Boy," George's favorite

Christmas song. Steve, a physical therapist by profession, set his guitar aside, put the bed railing down, reached over, lay on George's chest, and held him in his arms. Tears began. He went into the living room, sat in George's chair, and sobbed. In addition to sobbing for George, was he also remembering the death of his own father, his son's drug use, and his current divorce proceedings?

Steve and I both loved flowers, so we went outside and he cut several slips from flowers he would root and plant in his yard. I also gave him one of George's neckties and asked him to select a shirt. I was happy that a part of us would remain with Steve through these tangible forms. As he left, we both knew we would not be seeing each other as often in the future. It was a memorable visit.

In the afternoon, Carole, our chaplain at Regents Point, came and prayed with George and comforted me. She was more than a chaplain; she was our friend. We were so fortunate to have an abundance of caring people surrounding us. My friend Libby stopped by and offered to go get our mail for us. I would not leave George now, not even to get the mail. I felt an urgent need to be there at all times. Virginia and Bob ran an errand for me and stopped in to see George one more time. Over the past year, George and Bob had been developing a relationship. It was sad to realize that soon they would be friends only in spirit, yet I was so grateful that Bob and Virginia would remain in my life. Virginia and I had a deep bond despite being acquainted for only a few months. She was important to me as I released George, and she would be important to my future as I learned to live without him.

## Thursday, October 8

I awoke approximately every two hours to check on George. I wanted to be aware of when he took his last breath. My bed's position right next to his hospital bed made it easy to observe him. His breathing was shallow, but he was calm. His bedding wasn't disturbed, which was unusual since he had restless legs. Surprisingly, I felt calm.

That morning was day fifteen without food and the beginning of the third day without water. I called the Regents nurse and asked for morphine earlier than usual as I didn't want George to feel like he couldn't breathe. It was administered every four hours during the day. Hospice called and said someone would bring oxygen, as George might need that.

Several of our Regents nurses were from the Philippines. They told me that caregiving was a part of their culture and that care for the elderly was especially important. I relished our conversations and every contact they had with George. Some were tearful knowing George was leaving soon.

Our son-in-law Stevens visited and was a great comfort to me. He spoke to George, telling him of his love and respect, then prayed and, lastly, sat with me to discuss several issues. We hoped to have a memorial gathering shortly after George's death for the immediate family at

William R. Mason Regional Park, which borders Regents Point. We'd have to practice physical distancing and wear masks. The virus pandemic threw everything off-kilter. We'd have a celebration of life later when groups were once again allowed to gather.

The oxygen arrived, but the machine was so noisy that I hoped we didn't have to use it often. It was here in case George became agitated and couldn't breathe. At this point, the morphine was sufficient. He breathed, then gave a long pause, then breathed again. He was calm and hadn't moved his body in twenty-four hours. When he opened his eyes, he stared and didn't appear to focus.

I couldn't seem to wrap my head around some things. I continued to have ambivalent feelings about enjoying any activity or conversation while my husband was lying in the next room, barely breathing, and was, in fact, taking his last breaths. How was it that I could enjoy anything? I felt almost outside of myself that evening as I filled out the mail-in ballot for our national presidential election. Voting was important to me, yet it seemed trivial and intrusive while I was losing my husband.

## Friday, October 9

During the night I lay in bed listening to George's breathing. I awoke three times to check on him and decided to stay up at four o'clock, after getting six hours of sleep. That would be sufficient. Our darling daughters and Stevens would arrive that afternoon. Hospice would come soon.

That morning George's breathing was rapid. He was very warm, feeling feverish, so I put wet, cool cloths on his forehead. I washed his face, cleansed his mouth with a citrus-flavored swab, held his hand, and gently rubbed his arms. I told him once again that I loved him and I thanked him for all the good he'd done in this world, including being a good father and husband. I was so grateful that he was here at home with me and I was intimately involved with his care.

At 7:30 a.m. a Regents nurse gave George morphine. It was day sixteen with no food and day four with no water. He breathed forty breaths per minute and had a temperature of 103 degrees and blood pressure of 100/71 and descending. We had to turn the oxygen machine on with its unappreciated drone that negated our restful classical music. But if it eased George's breathing, it was beautiful.

George liked me in skirts, so I wore one that day, as well as a necklace and earring set that he gave me. I opened the window shutters in the bedroom, pushed them aside, and looked at the world beyond this room of death. I also lit a candle and placed flowers from my garden on the dresser. I doubted that George was aware of any of this, but it helped me.

Our hospice nurse arrived. She turned off the noisy oxygen tank and said it was no longer necessary. At 9:30 a.m. another dose of morphine was given, plus an acetaminophen suppository to bring down George's fever. I sat by his bed, laid my head next to his, held his hand,

and sang the song "Tell Me Why the Stars Do Shine" into his ear.

I sang the last words, "I love you," over and over. I watched his every breath. It became very shallow, then stopped. I glanced at the clock on the dresser; it was 11:15 a.m. George was gone.

I sat there beside him, for how long I didn't know. The nurse removed George's T-shirt and handed it to me. I wrapped it around my neck until all of George's warmth went out of it. She and Maria, the bath aide, washed George and put on a clean T-shirt and pull-up underwear. Then the nurse laid a blossom on his chest and said a prayer.

Joy and Stevens arrived soon after George breathed his last, Sonja came later, and the tears were ever present.

Hospice called the UCI Willed Body Program. An hour later the representative came, sat next to me on the couch, and gently spoke. He asked about George's death and about how I was doing. Finally, I asked if someone was coming to take George. He said he was there to do that and asked if he might bring in a gurney. His respectful manner comforted me. I joined him as he pushed the gurney into the bedroom.

"It is our custom to wrap the body in a shroud," he said. "May I do that?" With my consent, he began to wrap George. I felt compelled to assist him. It would be my last connection with George's body.

As we completed the wrapping, I cupped my hands around George's beloved head, kissed his forehead, and whispered a final goodbye. I covered his head with the shroud.

The representative picked up George in his arms and lifted him from the bed to the gurney. Stevens escorted them to the vehicle. The vehicle left. George left.

# *31.* A PARADOX

FOR SEVERAL NIGHTS I awoke every hour or two, just as I had when I cared for George. My brain was stuck on a habitual track, but George was no longer there—memories were. I cried, sighed, laughed, and smiled. I cried and sighed again.

A few days after George's death, I wrote this poem:

It is a Paradox.

George is gone. George is not gone.
He is gone from my sight. He is not gone from my
    inner vision.
His energy and love reach me from somewhere in
    the universe.

George's pale-blue eyes conveyed love and light.
The light went out last Friday. The love remains.

Memories bring sadness. Memories bring happiness.
I think of the difficult times. I savor the good times.

We lived together sixty years. Now I live alone.
I catered to his needs. Now do I focus on mine?
Is it okay to put the peanut butter jar where I want it?

We were a team, a two-some. Our team lost its star
  player.
How do I play the game as a one-some? A loner.

We were partners in parenting.
"Mom and Dad" our children said. Now, it's just
  "Mom."

I miss his habits. I don't miss his habits.
He liked things done a certain way.
It was unnecessary to lock the doors at night, he
  said.
Now I lock them.

I miss his gentleness. I don't miss his anger.
I miss his subtle sense of humor. I don't miss his
  ability to embarrass me.
I miss his soaring intellect. But not his searing
  intensity.

George was a man pursing justice for all.
Yet he, like I, could be unjust in his personal life.

We were two flawed people who never gave up on
each other.
Our love was as deep as the ocean,
With greater depth than our anger or disappoint-
ments.

I surrendered "he who loves me, and he whom I
love," into the arms of his Creator.
George is gone. George is not gone.

# *32.* ADIOS, GOODBYE, AU REVOIR, AUF WIEDERSEHEN

ONE DAY, NOT LONG after George's death, my mind drifted back to a music recital that I had attended a few months earlier. Two young women, university students, shared a piano bench and played the piano duet F minor Fantasia composed by Schubert, written shortly before his death at age thirty-one. The pianists explained that it consists of four parts, all seemingly Schubert's expression of saying goodbye to all the things he loved. The beauty of his rich music floated into my body and mind; it spoke to me, entering some of the innermost chambers of my thoughts. I pondered, with Schubert, the people and things I would miss as I left this earth.

Tender tears accompanied my thoughts, especially as I contemplated a farewell to my husband, our children, and our grandchildren. That final leave taking would be, well, so final. We experienced many separations in our long marriage, usually due to George's work. This separation would be different. There would be no "I'll call you when I get there." There would be no "I'll bring you a gift from my travels." Not even a "Don't forget to file our tax returns." The finality of the separation was difficult to grasp. Even if one believes in heaven, one's physical presence is still gone. And it is through that physical presence that we have related. We are body people.

One friend confided that after her husband's death, she even missed the things about her husband that irritated her. Another said that when his wife died, he missed the back scratching that had replaced sex in their later years. Yet another yearned for her husband's young self, the strong and protective man she married who made her laugh. That final adios will leave a trail of memories and longings.

In Norway, a deceased relative's tombstone was carved with the words *Takk for allt*, meaning "Thanks for everything." It seemed reciprocal: thanks to the deceased from the living, and thanks to the living from the deceased. One friend, a seminary professor who in the categories of saint and sinner lived heavily on the saint side, said as he was dying, "Forgive everything. Remember the best." At my death, those are the words I'd like etched on the mourners' hearts: Forgive everything. Remember the best. And thanks for everything.

George's death reminded me that my final day will come. But must I leave my children and grandchildren? The thought of a final au revoir pierces my heart. Though we raised our daughters to be independent, not needing to cling to their parents, in my illness and death I may want to cling to them. I will not want to let go. Have I finished being a parent? No. And our grandchildren, I can hear them call me MorMor, the Swedish word for "grandmother." I want to see them as responsible adults, as wise parents, as whatever. I want their hugs and affirmation of me to go on forever.

To say goodbye to all my extended family, as well as to my dear friends, sounds like a difficult and wrenching task. I think of how they have impacted my life. Many people have been to me like "God with skin on": they have comforted, guided, and partied with me. Best of all, they have loved me no matter what.

Beyond saying auf Wiedersehen to people, I think of just some of the things about life that I enjoy. Eating—what a pleasure! The crunch of almonds, the sweetness of tapioca pudding, the spicy tingle of barbequed chicken, the tang and saltiness of pickles—on and on. Oh, yes, the elegance of champagne, as well as the smoothness of a good Chardonnay.

I will miss nature's delights: The color of purple worn by violet, iris, and lilac blossoms. The aromas of sycamore trees, the ocean, and a field of alfalfa. I will miss the sounds of life: a drum, a hummingbird, and a loon on a Minnesota lake. And touch: The soft hairy coat of a dog or cat, the sharp edges of a sea shell, and the velvet of a baby's skin. I will sigh as I say farewell to these and countless other pleasures.

I don't have the talent of Schubert to compose music expressing my feelings about death. Neither do I have the writing talent to put such intense and deep thoughts into words. Fortunately, others have. Once again, I turn to the intimate writings of May Sarton that she included in her journal titled *Recovering*:

> I would like to believe when I die that I have given myself away like a tree that sows seeds every spring and never counts the loss, because it is not loss, it is adding to future life. It is the tree's way of being. Strongly rooted perhaps, but spilling out its treasure on the wind.

In the midst of contemplating death, may I truly live by sowing seeds that enrich the lives of the living. Perhaps by giving ourselves away, we are never really gone.

# *Epilogue:* I Need a Map

THE DAY AFTER GEORGE died, I awoke with a bewildering thought: What do you wear the first day after your husband dies? Where did that mundane concern come from? Was I a shallow person? A friend gave me some insight. She believed my question actually had profound meaning: I was asking how to be a widow.

In many cultures, widows wear black for a month, a year, or the rest of their lives. Widowhood defines their attire as well as their identity. I had never been a widow, but now that I am, I don't know how to be one. One thing I do know: I don't want my identity to be wrapped up—literally or figuratively—in grief.

At times I forget that I'm a widow. When I fill out forms, I automatically check "married." Then I remember. Am I really widowed? Single? This soon after George's death? Sometimes when I go for a walk, I check the time and quicken my step so I can hurry home to George. Then I remember, I have no need to hurry. I automatically add doughnuts to the grocery list. Then I remember, that was George's choice, not mine. New roles take time to comprehend whether it be because of marriage, divorce, diagnosis, or death.

George's death ended life as I knew it. I had been a spouse and a caregiver. Some who know me well claim I was George's caregiver for sixty years. My niece Amy, a psychotherapist, became a caregiver when her husband was diagnosed with a serious illness. She wrote, "Caregiving is such a powerful experience of letting go, then trying to grab on and live in the moment, but then finding the moment to be more than I can manage. The patience this demands of me is refining me."

Like Amy, I found caregiving, but also marriage, to be a powerful and refining experience. In times of contemplation, parts of myself were revealed to me. Now, would dwelling in the mystery of death and widowhood take me to another level of self-revelation? When George was living, I attended a caregivers' support group; now my involvement in a group for grievers aided my learning to live with loss.

George's death wasn't traumatic nor dramatic but a gentle slipping away, like a canoe skimming out into a placid lake, one paddle dip at a time. It was quiet and tranquil. That serves as a calm memory for me in my bereavement. Yet bereavement involves many other emotions: grief, remorse, joy, fear, gratitude, anger, and relief. Laughter may be the most surprising reaction, but it is valuable for its ability to lighten one's spirit. Our family loves to recount the funny things that George did. We laugh not out of disrespect but from pure pleasure. Our spirits dance in the midst of grief.

In trying to navigate my way as a widow, poet Jan Richardson provides some insights. She wrote in this excerpt from her poem "The Map You Make Yourself,"

You have looked
at so many doors
with longing,
wondering if your life
lay on the other side.

For today,
choose the door
that opens
to the inside.

Travel the most ancient way
of all:
the path that leads you
to the center
of your life.

No map
but the one
you make yourself.

While Richardson's words weren't specifically written for grievers, they work for me. I need to make a map. I pray for the courage to look within and then to develop a new route.

Will I have many more years of life? Maybe. Perhaps only a few. Nevertheless, I want to find meaning and purpose in this final road of life. With a map, I will put one foot in front of the other and step into the future.

I will be whole again, but I'll never be the same, nor do I want to be.

# *Acknowledgments*

THIS BOOK WOULD NOT be in existence without its subject, my husband, George. When he was well enough, I read aloud to him what I wrote. He had blinders on when it came to my writing; he always thought it was good and encouraged me to share it. I know he would be proud of me for bringing this book to fruition.

At times of boldness and bravery I sent copies of my writing to family and friends, as well as submitting them to the newsletters of our church and Regents Point. Based on the positive feedback I received, I was encouraged to continue writing. Here, I acknowledge and thank all those encouragers. You know who you are.

Thank you to Summit Run Press for publishing my words. Sharon Goldinger was the skilled editor who guided me in preparing the manuscript and in shepherding it to completion. Sharon and I worked together on a previous project, George's final book, *Silence Is Not the Answer.* I learned that I could trust her. When I sent my manuscript to her, I asked for honest feedback to which she replied, "When have you ever known me to hold back my comments?" I couldn't have done it without Sharon's expertise, attention to detail, and love of books, including mine.

ACKNOWLEDGMENTS

Support groups can be invaluable when going through a crisis. The two I attended, a caregivers' group and a grievers' group, provided information and encouragement. A shoutout of thanks to the members and facilitators.

I am grateful for the supportive care provided to George and me by the people from Regents Point Life Plan Community and by our hospice provider. Their help was indispensable in allowing us to remain in our home throughout his illness.

My family—immediate and extended—is my underlying rock. Your steadfast love secures and carries me.

# About the Author

VIVIAN ELAINE JOHNSON SPENT her childhood in a three-room house built by her father in Crystal Village, Minnesota. When she was an adolescent, the family moved to Minneapolis. It wasn't until she met and married George that she moved to what she thought of as exotic California.

Vivian completed a bachelor's and master's degree in behavioral sciences at California State University, Dominguez Hills, in addition to a two-year course in parish work at the Lutheran Bible Institute in Minneapolis. She lived in Sweden with her family for a year to do research and conduct interviews for her master's thesis, "Constructive Coping While in Bereavement," a comparative study of Swedish and US subjects. While there, she happily connected with her Scandinavian roots.

Vivian and George shared a spirit of adventure that led them to travel extensively. Many trips were to underdeveloped countries, where they briefly lived among those in poverty. They found such interactions educational and rewarding.

Vivian had the opportunity to interact with a wide range of people in crisis through speaking at universities, churches, and other venues; publishing articles on the subject of bereavement; and meeting with patients and family members through her work at the American Cancer Society.

In addition, Vivian was the cocreator of LifeStories, a communication game, and was commissioned to write the life stories of four Minnesota families that were published for their friends and families. She also wrote human interest essays for a variety of periodicals. This is her first book for the general public.

Her two grown daughters, Sonja and Joy, live with their families in Southern California. Vivian's five grandchildren call her MorMor, the Swedish name for "grandmother." One of the greatest losses for Vivian and the entire family was the death on Christmas Eve of her teenage son from a rare and aggressive cancer.

Vivian, who lives in Southern California, can be found tending potted plants in her home and on the patio, reading, writing, and enjoying either coffee or wine with friends. One of her favorite annual activities is spending a few days away on vacation with her two "darling daughters."

You can reach Vivian at vivianelaine0@gmail.com.